# THE
# MONEY
# DRUNK

# THE MONEY DRUNK

## 90 Days to Financial Freedom

Mark Bryan and Julia Cameron

Ballantine Books • New York

This edition published by arrangement with Lowell House.

Library of Congress Catalog Card Number: 92-90406

ISBN: 0-345-38130-0

Cover design by Dale Fiorillo

Manufactured in the United States of America
First Ballantine Books Trade Edition: April 1993
10  9  8  7

# CONTENTS

# AUTHORS' NOTE

We expect that you may recognize yourself, or perhaps a loved one, in these pages. This process of identification leads to healing and is an important aspect of our work.

Since many of the stories, traits, and classifications described are common, please be assured that all names, specific locations, and circumstances have been altered to safeguard the anonymity of those who chose to share their stories with us.

This book is intended as a solvency primer. You needn't be money drunk to use it effectively. You needn't be a member of what has come to be called the recovery community. The tools presented will also work for you even if you are already financially adroit.

# ACKNOWLEDGMENTS

We would like to dedicate this book to the Money Drunk who still suffers.

Additionally, we would like to thank:

Janice Gallagher, our editor, whose critical acumen, guiding hand, and brilliant number $2^5/10$ pencil were beyond price; our families and friends for their support; Ed Towle for his acuity and encouragement; the Reverends Mike and Sara Matoin, of Unity Church, Chicago, for their unflagging faith and generosity; Howard Mandel and Gayle Seminara of Transitions Bookstore, Chicago, for their early commitment to the project; Ginny Weissman for her early editorial support; Barry Cecconi and Dr. Sheila Flaherty-Jones for their therapeutic insights; Dr. Martin Block, Northwestern University, and Patrick Ryan, DePaul University, for their professional rigor; Sister Mary Julia Claire Greene, B.V.M., for her spiritual and journalistic assistance; Phyllis Estes for her enthusiasm; Michelle Lowrance for legal guidance and wit; Maureen O'Grady and Eli Hollingsworth for their eleventh-hour creative contributions; and especially our agent, Susan Schulman, for her expertise and astringent optimism.

"A wise man will desire no more than what he may get justly, use soberly, distribute cheerfully, and leave contentedly."

BENJAMIN FRANKLIN

# PART
# ONE

*THE PROBLEM*

# CHAPTER 1

FROM MONEY
DRUNK TO
MONEY SOBER

Let us be very clear: this book is not about giving up money. We're not against money. Anyone who says that money doesn't matter has never had to live without it, and we've had to live without it too often to be cavalier about the discomfort. All of us need money. Most of us would like to have more of it than we do. But more money is not always the answer; better use of it is.

Whenever we teach our Money Drunk seminars, we always joke, "Okay, who has the aspirin?" Everyone laughs but . . . invariably, the crowd meets us with crossed arms and frozen, skeptical faces. Even for a seasoned teacher it can be very intimidating to stand in front of so much anger and so much pain. We start our work. We watch them fidget, scoff, rage, get stomachaches, hot flashes—even tears. Looking at the room from across the podium we always take a deep breath, glance at each other for strength, and remind ourselves, "This is never easy."

But as we watch people move from denial and frustration into a hint of hope, their body language changes. The muscles in their faces loosen up. They uncross their arms, take a few deep breaths, start to relax. Then the laughter of shared experience begins as people identify with the questions we ask. We always remind them that we know the right questions because we had to ask them for ourselves. Slowly, our students come to believe that maybe, just maybe, their long years of confusion and pain about money will finally end. For the first time, viewed as an addiction, their money problems make sense. Like newcomers to Alcoholics Anonymous, they begin to feel free—even hopeful.

## ANATOMY OF A MONEY DRUNK

Throughout our lives, money was difficult. Mark's money problems started early. With parents who fought over finances and constantly fled bill collectors, he learned to view everything in terms of money.

As Mark says, "I had my first paper route when I was eleven years old, delivering the *Washington Post* to over a hundred subscribers. It was quite a job and now that I think back on it I don't know why an eleven-year-old would try to tackle that big a job, except that I thought we needed the money. I was probably right.

"From there I had a string of paper routes and then bagged groceries until an early marriage in my junior year had me working full-time to raise a family and going to night school. Even today it hurts me to see high school kids marry or try to raise children, because I know firsthand how hard it is going to be.

"But we tried our best. I went to night school and got a job in construction where I would meet the first in a string of abusive bosses whom I now realize triggered the 'reenactment' of my turbulent childhood. Needing the money badly, believing the boss's promises of promotion and bigger pay, I did not see how destructive and harmful he was.

"The important thing is that this pattern of making bad choices in jobs and working for abusive bosses and doing things I hated continued throughout what was to become my addicted twenties. I slid from one bad situation to another, always hoping for the miracle job or deal that would suddenly save me from the hopelessness of my financial situation.

"I worked eighty hours a week to be a restaurant 'manager,' making less an hour than the people I managed; I worked for others in construction trying to learn as I went; I worked all sorts of menial jobs for hourly wages, waiting for the foreman to see my potential, for someone to save me. But despite constantly working I never had any savings, owned a home, paid off a car, or even owned much furniture.

"By the time I was twenty-eight years old, quick money, big money had become the focus of my life. I had decided that money was the answer. I worked hard, nights as a bartender and days as a clerk at the Chicago Board of Trade, surrounded by successful people by day and by night. I watched the men at the board make millions and resented them for it, still waiting for them to give me a break, and at night I served them drinks and told them jokes, trying to be one of the guys.

"Then I got a high-paying job with the same hard-drinking traders. It was a lethal combination. I made thousands of dollars a week as a broker doing things for men who had gotten famous and rich doing them. I asked no questions; I just did my work and collected my pay. After all, I reasoned, I didn't invent the system. I was making great money; I was invincible.

"Then I lost my job for drinking. I was devastated. I hit bottom, hard. I lost everything. And I got sober.

"I had success in early sobriety. I finished college, went to graduate school, manufactured products in the Far East, lectured on business, and began to pursue a lifelong dream of being a writer for the first time since my youth. But my hunger for money continued to cause me problem after problem.

"I got my old job back and made good money for a while until someone offered a deal I couldn't—didn't—refuse because I thought it would make me rich faster.

"I got the opportunity to develop a new product. My new partner showed me how it would make me a lot of money if it worked, and he even had a few thousand dollars to pay me while I did it.

"My addiction to money blinded me to the reality of the situation, and I ended up selling four years of my work for those few thousand dollars and the promise of a big payoff some day.

"My new partner raged often. Reminding me of the violence of my childhood, he was also verbally abusive. He had 'given me the privilege' of working with him on his idea and I was grateful. Such was my self-esteem at the time. I borrowed from family and friends; I signed for a ninety-five-thousand-dollar loan.

"When I eventually went bankrupt after a series of disasters overseas regarding delivery of our product, I hit my financial bottom. After years of sobriety, the irony of going broke sober hit me right over the head."

As Mark would come to realize, he was re-creating the crisis atmosphere around money that he had experienced as a child. He was not able to dismantle that pattern of childhood dysfunction without help.

For Julia, coming from a financially secure home, money problems had emerged later in the form of what we have come to call financial anorexia. (Her story will appear in Chapter 7, The Poverty Addict). She has always found it hard to spend money on herself or to charge adequately for her work. For her—as for Mark—money, the lack of money, and the mismanagement of money had dominated and sabotaged her happiness.

## REVELATION

When we began teaching and writing together five years ago, not only was financial mismanagement the major problem for many of our students, but we also discovered that *we* both experienced a current of dis-ease around money that neither of us could quite explain. On the surface, all was well, yet we both felt subtly out of control. What was wrong, we wondered.

We became aware of our behaviors and attitudes about money. We underwent mysterious mood swings and realized we were either vague, euphoric, or depressive when it came to talking about money. It had an element of hype that both of us found toxic. What could we do about it, we wondered again.

At the time, both of us were involved with financial partnerships in which clarity was hard to come by. Our partners promised us the moon and delivered far less. Whenever we questioned their behavior too closely we were made to feel intrusive or guilty. If we pressed, emotional fireworks followed. Over time we found ourselves walking on eggshells, reluctant to encounter explosive dramatics on the job. There was a haunting familiarity to all of this for both of us. In a word, it felt like an alcoholic family. Our partners were out of control and we were enabling them to remain that way, by pretending their behavior (and ours) was normal.

"It's as if they're drunk or something," I told Mark one night on a long call during which we were, as usual, trying to make sense of our financial dealings.

"Money drunk!" I suddenly shouted. The minute the words were out, Mark and I knew we had a potential diagnosis.

For over a decade, we had worked on our own recoveries from addictive patterns. Julia had long taught creativity seminars in classes that included many recovering alcoholics and addicts, and for many years Mark had held in-hospital addictions seminars. As writers and teachers, we had worked with people in recovery from substance abuse, eating disorders, sexual addictions, and other compulsive behaviors. When it came to alcohol, drugs, food, or compulsive sex, we knew addictive behavior when we saw it. And now we were seeing it around money. Ours and theirs.

Well versed in addictions theory, we had the insight that a money addiction might present the same addictive patterns as an addiction to any mood-altering chemical and yield to the same treatment of awareness, acceptance, and action. These money behaviors made sudden sense viewed in terms of a binge cycle: tension, spending, relief, remorse, a period of abstinence or control, then tension, and the cycle begins again.

For us, the knowledge of the dynamic we were dealing with gave us immediate relief and clarity. We began to chart a way out for ourselves and our students. And it began to work. Soon, others came to ask us about their money problems. Because we were teachers, we started to teach.

We gathered tools from our extensive workshop experiences, from whatever addictions theory seemed relevant, and from sources as disparate as Julia's aunt Bernice, *The Diagnostic and Statistical Manual*-III-R (the handbook of modern psychiatry), and Benjamin Franklin.

## FROM MADNESS TO METHOD

This work, undertaken first for ourselves and later for others, enabled us to extricate ourselves from previously baffling and destructive involvements. Our own lives went from feeling mysteriously money drunk to feeling money sober. Working with others in our seminars and in private counseling sessions, we found our tools effective for them as well. We have written *The Money Drunk* in order to share our experience and our hope. Because we are teachers, we believe we can teach these principles to you.

We have interviewed, learned from, and taught hundreds of money drunks. We know unequivocally that we have identified the problem and mapped a way out.

For ourselves, we have watched our incomes double. We've

enjoyed the establishment of solvency and the gradual repayment of debts. We have seen the focus of our lives change to serenity and fulfillment instead of the former money madness that left us no peace.

To cite a few specific examples, we can sit in a room and discuss wages calmly. We can negotiate wisely and fairly, having learned to avoid ambiguity. Having lost the compulsion to spend, we know how to get several bids for a job and make the wisest purchase. (This alone has saved us thousands of dollars.) We have also learned how to say no when a project doesn't suit us.

By consistently keeping exact track of where our money comes from and how we spend it, we have learned to care for ourselves *now*, no longer waiting for the great day in the future when we will have enough to, say, buy new clothes, take a trip, get a decent car, have a savings account, enjoy hobbies, pursue our creativity.

Most important, we have begun to judge ourselves by our own standards, by our deeds instead of by our incomes or material possessions. We have also used our stories and those of many others to illustrate the many concepts of recovery we will present here.

In addition to the numerous personal stories used to illustrate the various disguises that money addiction may take and the effects of growing up in a money-drunk home, we will also define the different types of money drunks we have encountered—such as the Big Deal Chaser, the Maintenance Money Drunk, the Poverty Addict, the Cash Co-Dependent, and the Compulsive Spender—and show you what "the Way Out" looks like for each one of them.

We will also explore the deeply imbedded American misconceptions that help to make money so addictive: money as love, as success, as sex appeal, as security, as power, and finally, as God.

Some of you may be reading this book out of concern for

someone else. Some of you are worried about your own relationship with money. We would encourage you to go slowly in assessing your situation. Use this book to explore, not condemn, yourself or others.

Here you will find a broad spectrum of true stories that will allow you to recognize and identify the money-drunk syndrome in yourself or in a loved one. Hundreds of money drunks have contributed to this work. Many of them were still in denial. Their stories, like their lives, were filled with pain and confusion. Others followed the way out and were rewarded with peace and newfound financial freedom. The following quote is from a letter we received from Kathleen, a former student:

> I thank you for classes which challenged me to keep moving on this. . . . I have been recording, nonjudgmentally, every cent I have spent since we were assigned that exercise in early 1990. My husband started noticing how I seemed to have money left over at the end of a budget period; he started recording his expenses, too. At the beginning of 1990 we were several thousand dollars in debt. By the end of 1990 we were almost debt free and managed a fabulous vacation to Ireland. By April 1991 we owed nothing to anyone and were able to make a down payment on a home of our own. Last month we moved in! We do not know how this tool works, and we don't *want* to know. We plan to keep using it.

You may find it hard to read this book. It is easier for most people to talk about their sex lives than about their money. Do not let that discourage or deter you.

Like our students, you may suddenly become sleepy, space out, or develop a stomachache, a headache, or a pain in the neck. Alternatively, you may completely forget what you are doing and become numb, or suddenly find yourself furious—barking across the room at your wife, your husband, or even your boss. This displaced anger is very common. What you are really angry about is the wreckage and confusion of your financial affairs, and this anger will pass.

## HOW TO USE THIS BOOK

We will be guiding you through two important processes at once: First, we will be teaching you what the money addiction is, who has it, how to recognize it, and how to break through whatever denial you may have about it.

Second, we will be helping you lay the groundwork for recovery, setting your life on a course toward solvency and financial freedom.

If you will work with the tools in this book for 90 days, we promise you increased financial clarity and emotional relief. First read the main body of the book so that you may understand the basic concepts and the types of money drunks, then start at the beginning of the simple activities suggested and follow our program, week by week, day by day for 90 days. The basic program works for every type of money drunk, but occasionally we will introduce specific modifications for each type.

You do not need to understand why it works. You simply need to use it. If you do, we promise you will realize a future of hope and health and solvency.

Has your life been unmanageable because of money? This book will help you to determine your problem areas—and show you a way to get sober.

# 2

## THE "DRUNK" IN MONEY DRUNK

Do you know this man? Daniel doesn't want to answer the phone. He's afraid to go to certain parts of town. He crosses the street to avoid meeting friends. He's ashamed to take a cab, buy clothes for himself, or eat in a restaurant. Because he owes people money, Daniel feels guilty about even taking care of himself, avoiding friends and family along the way. His wife thinks he's cheap, and she never knows where the money goes. But Daniel says he is doing the best he can. He is: he's a money drunk.

If he's got it, he spends it. If he wants it, he buys it. He needs it, he tells himself. Frivolous buys become a necessity and everything that's necessary takes second place. There's not enough money to go around. Even when Daniel doesn't have it, he spends it anyway. He borrows it. He gets an advance. He asks for a loan. He says he'll pay you back. And he means it. He just forgets or "isn't able" to pay his debts.

Have you met this woman? Pamela steals from her husband's wallet and hides her shopping bags till he's in a "better mood."

She fibs about mysterious emergencies, small household catastrophes, that took her cash. She borrows her children's birthday money, raids next week's grocery money. She hoards a secret cache of bills she'll show her husband, "later." Pamela is a money drunk.

Many money drunks, unable to diagnose that a "money addiction" is at the root of their difficulties, have come to think of themselves as losers, outcasts, bad, or weak-willed people. Other money drunks, caught in their own self-will and denial, continue to claim they are only pursuing the American Dream and what is "due" them. They feel entitled to self-indulgence—even when it is killing them.

Dorothy, a compulsive buyer and spender, shudders with anxiety at the thought of *not* shopping. She often buys unneeded clothes that are inappropriate to her lifestyle. She buys where she can get credit, not where she can purchase what she wants.

An unwanted blouse may seem like a small error, but it paves the way to the larger ones, the ones like the unwanted couch that she lives with and loathes. Dorothy's habit of unconsidered buying extends from the small to the large—from the impulse buy at the checkout counter to the purchase of a bad car at the lot that "gave" her credit.

In the chapters that follow we will explore other types of money drunks. If you do not identify with the three short anecdotes above, you may find yourself in chapters five through nine.

## PORTRAIT OF A MONEY DRUNK

For money drunks, money is a mood-altering chemical. We binge to better our self-worth. We splurge for a temporary high. We spend lavishly so someone will like us, so we'll like ourselves. We abuse our credit lines, feel bad about it, and then buy ourselves a treat to feel better. We reenact our childhood programming about money.

We become spectators, not participators, in our lives. As binge-spending money drunks, we may buy a VCR to watch movies and forget about our dream of someday writing one.

Alternatively, we poverty-addicted money drunks feel we cannot afford a loaf of good French bread and so lose sight of our dream of a trip to Paris. Money is somehow spiritually "dirty." Poverty is our reactive addiction.

Dreaming of the life we'll have "when," most of us money drunks tune out on the life we've got now. Children become distractions. Wives or husbands become nags. Responsibilities become nuisances. Who has time for such details? We act as though money is love and love is money.

The money addiction, like alcoholism, is a disease of isolation. Many practicing money drunks are afraid to share the details of their reality. Afraid to let anyone know how we are *really* doing, we often begin to drop out, to isolate ourselves.

We money drunks expect money to do something more than pay our bills. We want it to fill our lives with happiness. Often unhappy people with low self-worth, we use money to *feel* different about ourselves. Either we overspend, buying ourselves things, or we underspend, buying ourselves "virtue."

This mood-altering relationship to money continues no matter how much money we may have. In "lace or disgrace," we are still focused on finances. Practicing money drunks want to be somebody special because we don't realize we're somebody special now.

We may not feel like enough because we are comparing ourselves to the people we see every day on television (the richest, the smartest, the most famous . . . ). This is what is classically called "comparing our insides to other people's outsides."

Whether we overspend or hoard money, we are still money drunk. Just as with the alcoholic, there is no *typical* money drunk. You'll find us in the glitzy, high-tech penthouse, supported by credit cards. We're in the house trailer with the color

TV, microwave, and the compact disc—all bought on time. We live in the suburban ranch house with central air, heated pool, and an empty two-car garage (empty because we're both working two jobs to keep it all up).

With no savings in the bank and no emotional solvency around spending, we make purchases from a position of weakness. They "let" us buy something. They "gave" us credit. In truth, merchants are happy to sell anything, any way that they can, but the money drunk seldom sees that. The need to spend, coupled with low self-worth, creates an inappropriate sense of gratitude to the credit merchants. We are thrilled when they give us a credit card and charge 18 percent interest for the privilege.

Ours is an addictive society. We admit that. We talk about alcoholism as our national problem. We urge our children to "just say no" to drugs. America's sweet-tooth, our acknowledged candy habit, has given us all the "sugar blues."

We seem addicted to everything that kills our pain, from junk food to junk TV. We have a "habit"—instant gratification. We overdrink, overdrug, overeat, oversex, and use TV to medicate the loneliness that's left. And yet, even with all of these addictions in motion, the money addiction may outstrip them all.

Money is an addictive substance for many people. As such, it holds all the potential for damaging lives and taking a toll on loved ones of any addictive drug. Like alcoholism and sex, food, or gambling addictions, the addiction to money is progressive, has its roots in self-esteem issues, and results in a downward spiral.

We would suggest holding one guiding idea: An obsessive-compulsive relationship to money exists whenever money is a ruling principle that has become destructive to career, family, and a sense of self-respect.

Many people, hearing the phrase "money drunk," may not know how literally we mean it. In our experience, we were *drunk*.

*By this we mean just what it sounds like: tipsy, giddy, out of control.* Intoxicated by our cash in hand or ready credit, we went on benders. We acted—and acted out—in ways foreign to our sober selves. We often even *felt* dizzy, or light-headed. And sometimes the "hangover" of remorse could be awful.

We are chemical beings, a system of intricate hormonal, adrenal, and pulmonary interactions. All of us have experienced a "flood of rage," a "dry-mouthed fear," a "wash of terror," or a "heart-pounding" panic. These are chemical reactions.

"I did not know how physically addicted I was to spending until I stopped it. The heart-hammering high, the agony of remorse, was the same biochemical roller coaster for me that alcohol had been for my sister," says Cassie, a commercial artist and a recovering money drunk. "When my sister got sober in AA, I was shocked by how much prettier she soon looked. When my money addiction was finally arrested, my sister complimented me on *my* looks for the first time in years."

For the recovering money drunk, the most persuasive evidence of the chemical basis for the addiction is the symptom relief we often experience once the illness is arrested. Many physical ailments from migraines to insomnia mysteriously disappear or are greatly alleviated as we become solvent. "What did you get? A facelift?" a friend might ask, as the mask of chronic worry vanishes from a recovering money drunk's face.

The physical transformation of many recovering money drunks is nothing short of astonishing. "What are you doing?" friends might ask. The answer is, it's what we're *not* doing that makes the difference. For many years, the biochemical basis of our behavior had dominated our lives. Often unconscious, always mysterious, we underwent a battering pendulum of stress and addictive attempts at stress relief that left our bodies and minds overtaxed: accustomed, indeed addicted, to rapid and extreme hormonal changes. With the addiction arrested, such mood swings often begin to subside.

Commonly, the addiction may take several forms: big deal chasing, maintaining an arbitrary standard of living, compulsive spending, compulsive non-spending, co-dependency on another person with the money addiction, and/or simple inability to live a full, happy life because of a chronic preoccupation with money and debt.

Taken in isolation, no single behavior announces itself as a surefire indicator of the money addiction. Clustered together, however, the behaviors begin to add up.

The important point is simply that we are dealing here with a recognizable disorder that can be diagnosed and arrested.

But first you have to admit you have it.

Money drunks can (and do) recover if they will follow a simple program of awareness, acceptance, and action. Awareness can often begin with answering a few simple questions.

## ARE YOU A MONEY DRUNK?

The diagnosis of a money addiction is a highly personal matter, but short, straight-to-the-point questioning of ourselves can often be an effective aid in self-diagnosis. We hope that the following characteristics (and others listed throughout the book), which detail common addictive patterns, will prove helpful. If you exhibit as few as any four of the following characteristics, chances are you are money drunk and can benefit from our 90-Day Program.

### Money Drunks:

1. Have their moods drastically changed by money.
2. "Act out" in other addictive ways because of success or failure with money.
3. Frequently argue about money.

4. Buy things and hide them.

5. Find it difficult to discuss their true financial status.

6. Frequently worry about money.

7. Buy things they cannot afford.

8. Lie about how much money they make.

9. Frequently borrow ahead on their paycheck.

10. Contract for new services they don't have the money to pay for.

11. Find it difficult to request payment for their work.

12. Choose (or reject) a lover because of his or her financial status.

13. Often face the final notices and threat of loss or actual loss of basic services such as lights, gas, food, insurance, shelter (eviction).

14. Are often rich and still worry about money.

15. Manipulate their creditors.

16. Avoid people to whom they owe money.

17. Avoid balancing their checkbooks.

18. Stuff their bills into drawers or throw them away.

19. Lead a restricted life because of their financial problems or their obsession with material gain.

20. Get sad or angry when discussing money.

21. Expect special treatment when unable to meet their financial obligations.

22. Come from families with money troubles or have at least one sibling with money troubles.

## BECOMING SOLVENT

The sober use of money is one of the most important skills a person can have. It can make the difference between living a good life and living one of constant struggle. Yet most of us receive little or no training for this life skill.

Being "good with money" is thought of as a knack, a gift, a mystery. A talent for money management is seen as "good luck" and seldom as a learned skill. Most of us would "like to be better" with money, but how to do that eludes us.

Many Americans could not financially survive a catastrophic illness. More than 30 percent—over 75 million Americans—have no health insurance or health care benefits. It is even estimated that the majority of Americans have a negative net worth because of their debt load. We contend that the mere lack of money is not the only reason for these financial shortfalls. As much as the lack, it is often the misuse of money that cripples an individual.

Our goal is solvency: the return of choice, sanity, and personal dignity in the use of money. More than a positive bank balance, solvency is a balance in our lives as a whole.

Solvency is a feeling of being comfortable with money—not anxious about it, and not careless with it, either. Solvency is a confident feeling of being prepared for any circumstance, of living within our means at all times.

Solvency means decisions aren't agonizing. Solvency means that one can take or leave most purchases. Nothing is a desperate "must-have." Yes, in solvency there will be things you may want, but they will cease to be things you have to acquire to soothe your psyche, medicate your wounded ego, or assuage your guilt for not feeling "good enough." Solvent, you will know that money cannot fill an empty soul. Solvent, you will find your soul less empty and your life more full. Freed from your addiction to money, you will find yourself.

# CHAPTER
# 3

## THE LAST OF
## THE
## ADDICTIONS

Just as an individual money drunk may be skilled at hiding the progression of his or her financial chaos from others, the addiction itself is often masked by another, more obvious, addiction.

All alcoholics are not money drunks and all money drunks are not alcoholics. Many people who don't have any other addictive behaviors *at all* still have the money addiction. But someone whose alcoholism is full-blown may blame his money problems on his drinking only to find that when he sobers up the money problems persist. Chances are, *that* alcoholic is also a money drunk.

Someone with a drug or food addiction may think of his or her trouble with money as the wreckage of another "presenting" addiction and not see the money addiction clearly as a problem in and of itself. Ironically, our obsessive-compulsive relationship to money is often the last addiction we recognize, although it may underline and inaugurate problems with all the others.

All too often, people in recovery from addictions to drugs, alcohol, or food keep waiting for their money problems to fall into line, only to find that they are consistently thwarted in their attempts to get solvent. This is the money addiction at work.

(A note for skeptics: It does not matter whether you accept the idea that the money addiction is really an addiction at all. The fact is, when money problems are recognized and treated as such, rapid and potentially permanent improvement follows. Try to keep an open mind and do not get caught up in the debate of addictions theory; finish reading the book and use the tools as designed. The results will speak for themselves.)

As any recovering addict will tell you, the real addiction is to changing our mood. This is why some of us can switch addictions like television channels. Any mood-altering thing can become addictive for us. As anyone experienced in addictions treatment will tell you, the addictions often rotate their time in the spotlight. As human beings, we all experience strong feelings. As addictive beings, some of us medicate them with our drug of choice, or with our compulsive behavior of choice.

It is common knowledge for recovering sex and love addicts that as soon as their sexual compulsions are put in check their finance and career issues come sharply into focus. And this unmanageability with money can trigger any of the other addictions unless it is dealt with.

In other words, often our money-drunk benders also set us up for a binge on alcohol, drugs, junk food, or addictive sex. Out of control with money, we spin further and further out of control in other areas of our lives. Is it any wonder we fail to diagnose our money troubles correctly?

Let's look at an example of how addictions intersect each other. Since the majority of people we teach are recovering from addictive patterns of some sort we have had many opportunities to discover how one addictive pattern triggers another. The story below might prove valuable for those of you who are (or fear you may be) multiply addicted.

## TIM'S DIET

Tim is a construction foreman, a compulsive overeater—and a money drunk. His is a binge mentality: "Blow it out with a big high."

A quiet, artistically gifted child, Tim was overwhelmed by family violence. At a very early age, he began overeating, literally putting a buffer of flesh between him and his feelings, between him and his family's anger.

With the family finances always out of control, the family endured crisis after crisis. In fact, crisis became normal to Tim. Instead of eviction being an exceptional, almost unimaginable event, it became a routine in the family.

"Just another night move," the family joke ran.

Whenever he got away from home for any extended period of time, Tim's weight and his finances would begin to stabilize. He would work hard, work out hard, and begin to feel like a "new man." But the money-drunk time bomb was always ticking away. When his feelings became too uncomfortable, Tim would overspend and then overeat.

Tim's tax refund would be spent on a day at the track, bingeing on junk food, fries, sodas, hot dogs, corn dogs, candy. Sickened by his spending, sickened further by his overeating, Tim would start with "What's the use?" and go on to finish the bender.

Feeling like a failure, money drunks often act like one. The nice new friend is too good for us. We may botch the lucky break we feel we don't deserve. We may cancel the needed job interview. We stop participating. We back away—from people, from family, from expectations, from plans. And ultimately, from hope, as Tim did during a binge.

"I don't understand it," Tim would say to himself. "I knew better." And he did, but knowing better did not help him fight his compulsion. Just as with alcoholism, self-knowledge is not the answer. Willpower, in the ordinary sense, seems to be useless.

It is very important for Tim to see himself as the money drunk who sets up his relapses on his food program. His addictions to money and food go hand in glove. Tim's denial keeps him from seeing them both.

## THE DEMON OF DENIAL

We anticipated that money addiction, like any addiction, would involve denial. We had listened to drunks still shaking from their bender as they explained it away and planned their next one. We had watched drug addicts use every possible evasion to continue with their addiction: "I knew it *would* hurt later so I took the pain medication early. . . ."

To our surprise, we found that the denial involved with money addiction outstripped them all.

"Everybody has debts."

"It's the American way."

"Once I get the cards down, I will be okay."

Any sentence on spending that begins with a "but" is worth looking at: "But I paid the cards off and I was just young, just depressed, just breaking up with John (or Mary). . . ."

Money drunks often perversely spend to celebrate because we've saved. To our skewed ear, all the ways sound within our (devious) means. We pay off our cards and then run them up again to congratulate ourselves. We say we won't, we know we shouldn't, but . . . we do.

Money drunks tell ourselves that everyone spends drunkenly once in a while—and perhaps everyone does, *once in a while*. What money drunks have trouble admitting is that our abuse of money is a yearlong, lifelong pattern. Whether we chronically overspend or underspend does not matter.

Most money drunks hate to admit we might be mentally and spiritually different from normal spenders. As money drunks, our financial careers are often characterized by frequent and futile and failing attempts to control (and enjoy) our money.

We money drunks promise ourselves never to bounce another check, open another credit line, borrow any more money from friends, or buy anything else that we don't need.

We are not people who would intentionally hurt or disappoint our friends or family. And yet, in the throes of the addiction, we often do just that. "If I ever get as bad as my brother, I'll have to do something," we might say, or, "My spending is a drop in the bucket compared to my sister's. She's got using her cards down to a fine art."

Pointing the finger is a favorite money-drunk pastime. We just don't point it at ourselves.

Overspenders are not the only money drunks who fib to themselves. Poverty-addicted money drunks do it, too. If anything, they do it the best of all.

Money addiction and food addiction are very parallel. Just as anorexia often goes undetected because of our "you can't be too thin" culture, financial anorexia easily masquerades as virtue, as a reaction to our rampant materialism.

"I call it the Catholic Girl Syndrome," Julia used to joke. She was making light of her financial anorexia, trying to "blame it on the nuns" who had taught her young that sacrifice was a virtue that gained her brownie points in heaven. "I can always spot an ex-Catholic schoolgirl," she claims. "We're the ones in baggy black or navy blue—just like those uniforms we hated!"

Don't try to tell Julia that religion has nothing to do with her clothing choices: early convent chic, via the Catholic Charity Thrift Shop. Don't try to convince her, even gently, that her self-denial was unhealthy. Self-denial was her anorectic self-image. She got high on martyrdom and called it virtue.

Most of us money drunks tell ourselves soothing little lies to cover up the big one: that our relationship to money is toxic and we know it. "I really needed it," the compulsive spender justifies her latest purchase: winter scarf number nine.

"I'll subscribe next year," the underspender promises, cheating herself of a year's reading on the hobby she loves.

"I'll pay him both rents on the first," says the Big Deal Chaser, waiting for the Big Payoff, "At least I'm not on welfare."

## TERMINAL VAGUENESS

Over and over, we are struck by the "selectivity" of the money-drunk memory. We have come to believe that financial amnesia is a blocking device used to evade pain. We call it "terminal vagueness."

"I don't remember getting that bill."

"I can't remember, but I think I paid him back."

"Did I get a final notice?"

To the non–money drunk, such vagueness is infuriating—and even suspect. "How can they not know?"

We have come to believe that stress creates a kind of screening process by which disturbing details are set aside. And for a money drunk, "disturbing details" involve money.

Paid on a Friday, Doug, a musician, impulse buys four new albums he doesn't need. He "forgets" the notice from the gas company and is short the funds to keep his service on. He spends a weekend eating cold cereal until he can borrow money on Monday to restore his service.

When Doug told us this story, he did not really see cause and effect. Like many money drunks, he was out of touch with the realities of "money out/money in." The concept of "If you don't spend it, you'll still have it" eluded him.

Denial is the hardest mask to remove because we are hiding

from ourselves. Reality often eludes us, lie by lie, because we are constantly maintaining our "happy face," never really willing to look into the mirror beyond our own facade. This denial mechanism keeps us out of reality. And soon our fantasy of financial manageability comes crashing down.

## HITTING BOTTOM

Some money drunks hit bottom when we still have houses and cars. Some wait to wake up until we're homeless, evicted by our last landlord for our last bad check.

This moment of clarity, of awakening to the truth, is called the "bottom." And the bottom is a feeling—not a place. It is a feeling of surrender, of "I can't take this anymore." And some of us must be in more pain to hit bottom than others. Like the old joke in AA, "Alcoholics come from all walks of life. From Yale to jail, from Park Avenue to park benches," money drunks too have different tolerances for pain.

Suzie, a financial planner, hit what might be called a "high bottom." She had a house, a car, a good credit rating; what she didn't have was an okay for a new loan she was seeking. The balance between her debt load and her income level made her a poor risk, the bank told her. Suzie, more willing than many to face the music, admitted to herself that they were right. Her debts had been steadily increasing. Her earning power, eroded by her anxiety over her finances, had steadily decreased. Suzie went for help.

Not all of us get the message so easily.

Sara, a creative writing teacher, recalls her money-drunk days with intense remorse. "I wish I could say that I hit my bottom early, but I didn't. Years before I entered recovery, I sat on the floor of the expensive brownstone apartment I had rented in a posh New York neighborhood.

"My five-year-old daughter sat beside me. Between us was a large pressed-glass jar. Our penny pot. It was the last money I had left to feed my child, to feed me; the only money left, after paying for the necessary extravagance of my outsized rent, and upscale lifestyle.

"My daughter was just learning to count. 'One . . . two . . . three . . .' She jumbled dimes and pennies together trying to help.

"The shiny ones are worth more," I told her. I tried not to say it with any irony.

"Shiny things had always seemed worth more to me. I had a great address, in a great neighborhood. I had original lithographs on my walls and Laura Ashley sheets. I even had a designer chair, overstuffed and overpriced, which I sold to my upstairs neighbor for a month's groceries.

"Now, I am in recovery. Sometimes at the end of the month, when cash is running low, my daughter will remind me, 'Remember when we ate out of the penny pot?' or, in a worried little voice she will ask me, 'Will we have to eat out of the penny pot again, mom?'"

Sara tells her daughter that the worst is over and that they have survived it. She tells her that things will get better because she, Sara, is getting better. And she tries to remember to tell herself that she is lucky to have hit a bottom at all and lived through it. We have found case after case in which money drunks do not survive hitting bottom.


## THE MOMENT OF CLARITY

It has long been known that suicide is often linked to alcohol and drug abuse. The overwhelming majority of all violent crimes can be linked to alcohol as a precipitant. It is our feeling that the money addiction is often an invisible precipitant as well.

A woman in Champagne, Illinois, sought help for her money addiction after finding her spouse dead, with a list of their debts and his credit cards left as his suicide note.

In Michigan, a father plunged his car with himself, his wife, and their three children aboard into a swift-flowing river. It was an act "To escape my burdens," he said. The burden? Thirteen thousand dollars in family debts. The children perished. The father survived to face not only his debts but what he did because of them. His wife survived to try to live through the grief and anger.

Remember the famous window jumps of 1929? Those were people with nothing in their lives to live for once the money was gone. In that empty space, when someone stands alone in despair, money drunks must often choose between annihilation and surrender. Either they try suicide, in a final, permanent gesture of defiance or they give up, and ask for help.

Finally defeated, drowning in despair for lost dreams, a money drunk hits bottom. Or the bottom hits us with bankruptcy or eviction. Bad as it feels, admitting that we are losing the fight is our first victory—because we have become teachable.

The truth that we need help has finally managed to break through our shield of denial. Thank God.

Against all our attempts to avoid it, deny it, block it, lie about it, evade it, disguise it, rationalize it, or pretend it is otherwise . . . we have hit bottom. And we do not know it all. We need help.

No matter how we differ, all "bottoms" have two things in common. The first is despair. The second is anger.

Despair and anger. Anger and despair. For the money drunk, these are constant companions. Our despair tells us we are all bad—intrinsically, in our souls, bad. Our anger tells us that "someone" has done us wrong, treated us shamefully.

Facing our anger and despair, like facing the music, grows harder with every small delay. "You don't want to know," a money-drunk wife explains as she hides her finances from her husband.

"I'll handle it," the money-drunk husband assures his wife, when all he is really doing is letting his anger turn inward. This anger then becomes shame.

"Shame is what keeps you from you," a recovering money drunk explains. For a practicing money drunk, there's a lot that he might do . . . if only he weren't so ashamed.

Embarrassed by her mounting bill, Mimi avoids her health club, then hates her pillowy thighs.

Ashamed of his shoes, Marvin makes excuses to avoid business meetings face-to-face, or toe-to-toe. He deals by phone and loses business in the process.

Stricken with shame, we money drunks often sever or slowly relinquish the ties that are dear to us. Embarrassed—perhaps frightened—we avoid places and people where our shame might be brought to light, and this isolation leads us back to anger and despair in a very vicious circle.

Despair is the money drunk's secret self-hatred, the chant we wake to every morning: "You're worthless, you're stupid, you're a failure, you're a bum."

Early in recovery, it is critical that we acknowledge that our debting/spending/worry is an addictive illness, *not* a failing of character. And that the anger that we feel toward ourselves, toward everyone, is the fuel we will use to get better.

## A PREVIEW OF RECOVERY

In ourselves and others, we have found the symptoms of dysfunction around money run a debilitating and even predictable course. Beginning with behaviors that seem relatively harmless—the occasional kited check, the overdraft at the bank or credit-card spending spree—the addiction often progresses over time to become linked with more serious behaviors—the forged check, the faked financial records, the money borrowed from work without the boss's knowledge, the chronic bender at the track or at the shopping mall.

But, just as the addiction has a progression, perhaps starting with a few bounced checks and escalating into repossessed cars or furniture, maybe even eviction, the recovery has a progression too.

When we met him, Bobby, a civil engineer and a practicing money drunk, was having trouble in his business. His new projects didn't quite happen. The job opportunities never quite materialized. The promised paycheck was abruptly withheld. He began to run late in his rent, rarely at first, then often. He was just scraping by or borrowing it from friends. And this shame around borrowing money kept him from leaving the house. (In a chic neighborhood, of course.)

Month after month, Bobby went to his friends with yet another story of why he didn't have the money for rent, who'd let him down, when he would pay it. Month after month, the rent came later and later. And, month after month, the apartment he lived in grew shabbier. Good neighborhood or not, his place was a slum.

The paint began to peel. The carpeting became worn through. Even the plumbing began to fail. Bobby was afraid to complain. He felt he owed his landlord more than just rent. After all, his landlord knew his secret: that he was a failure. And all the while Bobby went deeper and deeper into debt.

For Mark, Bobby was a particular challenge. His high level of intelligence and his low self-worth combined to make him a particularly persuasive self-abuser. Mark worked long and hard with him to get him to stop judging himself and start altering the behaviors he was so judgmental about. Together, they arrived at Bobby's "Bottom Line" (see Week Four in the 90-Day

Program), a list of destructive behaviors that he would abstain from one day at a time.

As Bobby began to accrue some time "money sober," starting at Week One with Counting, his bouts of self-loathing began to slowly abate. Each week without a financial catastrophe strengthened his conviction that he could and would make a better life for himself. One bounced check due to a math mistake nearly sent him spiraling back into despair, but Mark reminded him it was progress, not perfection, that mattered. By changing his behavior first, Bobby was able to change his self-image second. It is our experience that the process cannot work effectively the other way around because denial blocks out the ability to act in our own behalf. And a little change in behavior (such as counting our money) goes a long way.

## THE DISEASE OF MASKS

The money addiction is a disease of masks. Do not be discouraged by feeling you've awakened a little late. Now you are aware and have a new set of masks to deal with. Just as other behaviors such as alcoholic drinking may have covered the money addiction, the money addict may also move from mask to mask within the addiction itself. A money addict may wear the mask of the Compulsive Spender, the Big Deal chaser, the Poverty Addict, the Maintenance Money Drunk, or the Cash Co-Dependent, and may periodically change one mask for another. Regardless of which mask the addiction wears, the play is still the same. And the addiction is still to money.

Many of us money drunks find we identify with multiple facets of the addiction. Going back over our personal histories we often discover that we have moved from one type to another to another much the same way an alcoholic might switch from wine to beer in an attempt to control his disease. The 90-day program is designed to work regardless of which mask your addiction may currently be wearing.

For a deeper understanding of these masks, we have described each of the "types" in detail in Part Two. For now let's see how growing up in a money-drunk home might influence the masks we choose.

# CHAPTER

# 4

## GROWING UP
## MONEY DRUNK

Many of us money drunks come from money-drunk homes. Often, finances have been a family blight for generations.

Think back to how your parents handled money: Did they have enough? Did they argue over it? Do you get the impression they didn't know much about it? Did they try to buy your love and respect?

As a money drunk, you may have the same attitudes (and actions) about money that your parents had. Alternatively, your attitudes and actions may be mere reactions, a swing of the pendulum far to the opposite of your parents' behavior. Miserly parents may produce binge-spending children while binge-spending parents may raise a crop of miserly offspring.

The point is that the money addiction may be inherited and that your attitudes and actions around money may need to be freed from early, negative conditioning. Regardless of the extent or type of this familial conditioning, the 90-day program will alleviate the problems that it has caused. Just as all alcoholics (whether wine drinkers, or beer drinkers, or whiskey drinkers, or binge drinkers, or daily drinkers) get sober the same way, money drunks of all types respond to a single basic recovery program. The stories that follow describe an array of cause-and-effect situations. While not meant to be complete, they will help you begin to recognize your own family background and how it may contribute to your current dysfunction around money.

## MONEY AS RESPECT

Ken comes from a home where his father worked two jobs, sometimes three, and his mother spent the money as fast as his dad could make it. His father never made enough to make her happy, and she regularly let him and the kids know it. More money meant more respect. If Ken's father could not earn "enough" with three jobs, is it any wonder that Ken came to believe that no ordinary amount of money could ever be enough for him? Driven by a desperation to have more—and therefore *be* more—Ken considered any normal paycheck inadequate to his outsized needs. Time and again he abused his steady job to pursue the windfall of a "big deal," the sudden riches with which even his mother could not argue.

While we would never say that this is the only factor in Ken's financial dysfunction, we believe that such early patterning is certainly pivotal. We have seen this too many times to ignore the obvious correlation between family patterns and subsequent financial failings.

## MONEY AS EVIL

Anna's family was the poorest one in a very rich section of a large midwestern city. She remembers never having the kind of privileges the other kids had, such as riding lessons, dance classes, new designer clothes. Her family's reaction to their relative financial duress was to make a virtue out of it.

Anna's mother and father taught their children the foolishness of money, that it was a vice not worthy of their time or attention. "There are more important things in life than money," they were told.

While this maxim is certainly true in some ways, in Anna's family it was used as a gloss for what Anna's parents obviously felt was a shortcoming. Instead of pointing their children toward genuine virtues, they educated them to avoid money as a vice.

As an adult, Anna still has trouble putting money in its proper perspective. She never learned that money is the just result for a job well done. As a result, she is chronically underpaid. She never learned that money could well be used as a means to a worthy end: a lovely dress for a special occasion, a lovely vacation after a grueling year.

Addicted to poverty and to the false sense of virtue it afforded her, Anna was miserly with herself and her dreams.

## MONEY AS LOVE

Jeanne grew up a sickly child in a prosperous home. Troubled by asthma and chronic allergies, she was frequently hospitalized during her childhood years. In order to make her feel better her parents would buy her treats—many, many treats.

Instead of reading to Jeanne in her long hospital stays or playing board games, instead of just sitting by her bed, her parents bought her teddy bears, stuffed bunnies, dolls of all shapes and sizes. Things to keep her company.

Growing up as she did in a home where presents were used in place of love, she now buys herself a present whenever she feels needy or unloved. This is often what Jeanne feels because she does not recognize love expressed in other ways.

Although she outgrew her allergies and asthma in adulthood, Jeanne has never outgrown her chronic need for treats, the extravagant expenditures that make her feel better. Now a happily married woman, she jeopardizes that marriage with spending sprees that tax her husband's patience and their income.

## THE WORKAHOLIC MESSAGE: MONEY *INSTEAD* OF LOVE

Jeanne's parents were a well-meaning couple who were simply unable to express their love for her without the intermediary of money. But other parents don't even have the time to try.

Another way that parents can set the money addiction in motion is the overtime crime: workaholism. The "I'm too busy working to be a parent" message teaches children that money can substitute for affection.

A child of divorce, Elise has a father who never comes to see her. When he wants to show his love for her, he sends his secretary to buy her something expensive. Instead of his time, he donates his money to see to it that his ex-wife and daughter have what they need. "Lots of kids don't get any child support," is an explanation that does little to comfort Elise. Her "divorced" friends have fathers who at least come to see them.

The last time Elise saw her father, he took her to an expensive restaurant with his expensive new girlfriend. He spent dinner telling the girlfriend about the time he took Elise on her class trip, eight years ago. "The one time he did anything with me," Elise says.

This year, Elise is attending a new school. She wants to fit in. She wants to be liked. She wants to be accepted as part of the gang. This is normal. What is not normal is that she feels she must use money to do it.

When her schoolmates ask for a loan Elise is afraid to say, "No. That's my baby-sitting money. I earned it. Earn your own." Instead she lends it out and then worries whether or not she will get it back. If money is what it costs her to earn her new friends' love, Elise is willing to pay that price. Even if it means she can't buy what she was saving for. Even if it means that in treating others specially she treats herself badly. "Come on, loan me a dollar," her new friend, David, teases her. "I'll pay you back. I'm rich enough for you to marry me." (David is 13, but already thinks marriage is a money issue.)

Elise is excited that David likes her. She doesn't like lending her hard-earned money, but she does it. Already she believes that money equals love.

Already, Elise is a potential money drunk, believing, "I am not likable by myself, just for being me. I will buy their love." She is an embryonic cash codependent.

## MONEY AS SOCIAL STANDING

Michael was a welfare-lunch-line child. His parents worked— and worked hard—but the family finances didn't. Michael's parents were Maintenance Money Drunks. They chronically spent their money on items they did not need and fell short of cash for the real necessities.

Instead of buying groceries for the home and packing sandwiches for school so that Michael could skip the embarrassing lunch line, his mother, meaning well, bought him the "Superman T-shirts that he saw on TV." It was a question of misplaced spending.

What Michael did not learn was priorities. What he did learn, even as a 10-year-old, was to dress for success and cover his feelings literally with whatever fashion craze was acceptable.

Michael never got told he was nice no matter what he was wearing. Michael never heard that the shirt didn't matter but he did. Michael heard what he was taught—that money mattered more than how he felt.

As an adult, Michael still believes that money matters more than he does—and certainly more than his feelings. A gifted man with a love of children, teaching, and history, he has ignored his dream of a degree in history to work on a factory assembly line and buy himself new cars, new TVs, everything but the new life he would really like, the life in line with his real dreams and not just appearances. Michael is carrying on the family legacy.

## MONEY AS BOXING RING

One way or another, children react to what they see. They begin this "reacting" very young and may carry the seeds of a money-drunk future before they reach their teens. If you come from a family that constantly fights over money, you may grow up believing that money matters more than a happy home life; or you may sacrifice yourself on the altar of "peace at *any* cost" and become a people pleaser, never standing up for what you want.

In Terry's family, the fights are always about money. Terry's dad wants her mom to stay home with the kids. He'll be the breadwinner. But what Terry's father really wants is control over their money and over his wife. And Terry gets the uneasy feeling that there is never enough money; she feels guilty about asking for anything.

Still a preteen, Terry is learning that money is entitlement. "I make the money! I decide how it's spent!" her father shouts. He doesn't want his wife to work "outside the house," but he controls the household money like an evil feudal lord. It is a home run by money and by fear.

Terry watches her mother preen and primp and plan when she wants the cash for something extra. She sees her butter up her dad, make his favorite dish, manipulate. Worse, sometimes she wants Terry to do the asking. "You ask Daddy," Mom some-times says. Turn on the charm. Be a people pleaser.

Terry is learning that men are a money machine, that women have to grease the wheels, and sadly, that money is power.

Lorraine grew up in a violent home where her father's rage drove her mother to make peace at any price. For years Lorraine watched as her mother cowered and acquiesced to her father's bullying and unreasonable demands in order that no one be hurt. Lorraine watched as her father drank and spent excessively and her mother made do. Lorraine focused on being a good girl in whatever terms her father defined it. "Do what your father asks," her mother would say, "You know how he gets if you don't."

As a successful adult woman, Lorraine finds herself unable to break her childhood pattern of peace at any cost. Conditioned by her father's rages to believe that all men are tyrants, she has difficulty saying no even when it is in her own best interests. This is nowhere more apparent than in her financial dealings. Time and again, as a Cash Co-Dependent, Lorraine has taxed her financial resources to loan money to deadbeat boyfriends or out-of-luck siblings.

"I'm such a soft touch," Lorraine complains. "I just can't bring myself to say no."

## MONEY AS TABOO

If we grow up in a family where money is taboo and seldom mentioned, money becomes shameful to us. We don't talk about it. We don't ask about it. We pretend that it can take care of itself or just go away. If we get in trouble with it, mismanaging it becomes our secret shame. This was Julia's dilemma.

"I should know that. I should know that," she chided herself.

But what she didn't know ranged from proper pricing for her work to what a money market account was. In her denial, Julia excused this as a sort of artistic "flakiness." What it was, she realized in recovery, was ignorance rooted in shame and masked by artistic arrogance: "Artists are like that."

They don't need to be.

For those who grew up with money as a taboo, financial concerns linger in their adult life as a constant haze of concern. Terminally vague about financial matters, these money drunks go through life with a sense of impending doom. Maybe they will have enough money, maybe not. They are scared to find out because money is taboo.

At 40, Mary, an artist, still doesn't know basic financial terms. She "keeps things simple," by cashing her paycheck at work, saving "under the bed." Mary is embarrassed to ask for good advice. She feels she "should know."

But how would she know? Raised in a family where money was never discussed, Mary married a man who "ran the show" for both of them. Although she worked, she worked for a "Big Daddy" company that encouraged dependency in its employees, calling it corporate loyalty. "Just stay with us and we will take care of you. . . ."

When the marriage ended and the job ended, Mary entered a terrifying new world where finances were something to be managed, not ignored. Despite great talent and experience in her field, Mary found herself ill prepared for the hard bargaining that the free-lance world requires. After years of valiant effort, she finally went under financially from a series of reverses and sheer exhaustion.

Mary, middle-aged, is back at home, living with her depressive mother, "to save money." Frightened by financial realities, she lives in a netherworld of her mother's making where money is still not discussed. In that gray world, Mary continues to feel like a child, like someone who must be taken care of, not like the competent adult that she is.

## MONEY AS SEX

Claire, a much-married money drunk and former model, grew up dirt poor but pretty in the sugarcane fields of Louisiana. Her father and mother worked in the canning factories for subsistence wages. She remembers not having enough money for her cheerleading uniform at her tiny country school. For her, a lack of money became a lack of self-worth, creating a sense of helpless anger at her circumstances and at the world. But Claire was happy when her boyfriend offered to buy her uniform.

As she grew into a beautiful young woman, the attention of the town's rich boys made her feel awkward, envied by other girls, and wonderful. Though she took much of her repressed anger out on these suitors, making them buy her things and take her to expensive places, she still loved the attention. When she was 20, she decided to move to the "big city."

In no time, she became a wide-eyed femme fatale, batting her eyelashes in the boudoirs of the rich and famous from Miami to New York. Photographs for magazines made her feel even more "entitled" to attention. And the kind of attention she liked best was money. Yet, the rich life felt cheap.

She struggled for many years with a sense of loss and hopelessness. Looking to "stay out of the canning factories," she allowed herself to be the mistress of rich men who spoiled her, and her idea of herself. Money-drunk sexual sprees leave a terrible hangover of shame behind them. She has yet to get over judging men by their wallet.

Like many money drunks, Claire equates sex and money. While she would be insulted if you suggested she could be had for a price, the truth is that she can't be had without one. (If the trip is expensive enough, how can she feel "cheap" sleeping with a man as a thank-you?) Claire considers herself a woman with high standards, but the gold standard determines her morals.

Raised to think of diamonds as a girl's best friend, many money drunks still believe that marriage is the route to financial security. Terms like "fortune hunter" or "gold digger" seem very harsh to describe what they might call "looking out for their own best interests."

For the money drunk who confuses sex with money (and both with love), "cash and carry" means that enough cash can carry a woman across the threshold. *Money-drunk men believe this, too.* And many money-drunk men feel sexually unworthy because of their poor financial situation.

Brian, a tool-and-die maker like his father, is afraid to ask Debbie, a legal secretary, for a date. She is pretty and funny and seems to like him, but "seems" is the word Brian centers on. After all, a girl as pretty as she must have her choice of men. And Brian knows he couldn't possibly afford to take her to the same places the other men could; he remembers, too, his mother always complaining about their being too broke to do anything.

Convinced that sex is money and money is sex, lacking the one, he figures himself a loser at the other. A Poverty Addict, he wears his poverty the way a pretty woman wears an extra 25 pounds—to remove himself from the running.

For many married money drunks, the symbiotic association of our self-worth with money follows us right into the marriage bed. A big paycheck equals a big payoff; cold hard cash entitles us to cold hard sex. Conversely, a week when we're low on cash may find us low on libido or greedy with neediness, angered that our right to "claim" sex has been threatened.

Entitlement often follows feelings of financial heroism. "I make good money; she owes it to me." Many money drunks let their relationships slide and do little to promote real intimacy outside of sex.

## MONEY AS THE FIRST LINE OF DEFENSE

In the case of an overachiever, it is less easy to spot the money addiction in motion.

Harper is a blond, handsome, multiply married multi-millionaire. He makes big money as a salesman, a super sales-man. Every month he must clear $30,000 in commissions just to make his nut. He does it.

We are societally conditioned to admire people like Harper. And well they should celebrate their accomplishments, but there is no monetary equivalent for joy. Too often these people are not happy despite their money. Never able to appreciate themselves, they remain driven long after money has taken them from their children, their spouses, and their dreams. Big shots to others, they are still children to themselves, trying to buy comfort for the wounded little child inside who still wants love and affection.

As a child, Harper was beaten physically and emotionally. He is haunted by his father's scream, "I pay the bills here." That scream rationalized the beatings and taught Harper that it was very important to make a lot of money—no matter what. His father made money and nobody ever beat *him*. For Harper, even as a grown man, money is all there is. Money was a way to stop the beatings.

All the decisions in Harper's life have used money as their only guidepost. His jobs, his lovers, his wives, his friends—all are chosen and maintained on the basis of how much they can contribute. He has blocked his own emotional needs for so long *with money* that he doesn't know any other way.

## FINANCIAL CARETAKING

Many money drunks find they have strong conditioning that tells them to stay quiet and "not rock the boat." Often from homes where dysfunctional parents forced them into feeling overly responsible for adult concerns, they grew up facing situations for their parents—and difficult situations at that.

Severely dysfunctional parents think nothing of hiding behind their children or using them as pawns. When the going gets tough, they send a child to do an adult's job: having the child talk to the landlord, or borrow money from other relatives, or sending them to the store for credit.

When these children grow up they become caretakers. They enable those they become involved with financially, and, just as they did as children, they often ignore their own feelings, blame themselves for other's shortcomings, or distrust their own perceptions if they sense that anything is "crazy." They may become overly responsible employees, the kind who get victimized and manipulated by unscrupulous employers.

Money drunks, like adult children of alcoholics (ACOAs) or children from dysfunctional homes, may repeat destructive patterns of becoming involved in business, romantic, or financial dealings with people whose actions and attitudes are resonant of our relationships with our parents or families.

All too often, raised in homes where appropriate boundaries were nonexistent, we have difficulties establishing boundaries in our business life as well. And just as we were often children made privy to information and emotional burdens inappropriate to childhood, so in our business lives we often find ourselves "helping out" bosses who are asking us to take on roles and responsibilities far beyond those of employee. We may trust others to have our best interests at heart when they in fact don't. We, as adults, may seek, on an unconscious level, the negativity, the invalidation, the distrust, lack of boundaries, overresponsibility, or overprotectiveness—even downright abuse—that we experienced as children. This can make for a maddeningly elusive financial state brought on by patterning we don't see.

If you have not found yourself in the preceding family examples, we would urge you to realize that it is possible you may be a money drunk despite a perfect childhood. There are many we have worked with who are from homes that have every appearance of normality. You may be too. You may be like the alcoholic from a home where no one drank and who cannot seem to find any childhood link to his illness—yet still must recover.

You will know intuitively if some problem in your family background has maintained an influence in your financial affairs. However, regardless of cause, we must now deal with the situation as it is and move on to inform ourselves about the various disguises the money addiction may take. Answer the following questions and then move on to Part Two, in which present day behaviors, engendered perhaps by childhood experience, are explored.

## DID YOU GROW UP MONEY DRUNK?

1. Did your family believe that the rich got what they have: By screwing over someone? By cheating someone? Because their family had money? Because they are lucky? Because they stole it? Because they are morally bankrupt?

2. Did your family believe that money was evil?

3. Did your family feel that poverty was morally superior?

4. Did your family resent the poor?

5. Have you ever traded sex for financial security?

6. Have you ever decided not to ask someone out because of your financial status?

7. Did your parents fail to teach you useful tools for managing money?

8. Did your parents physically fight over money?

9. Was money a taboo subject in your family?

10. Was money a family secret?

If you answered yes to any two of these questions, you may have grown up money drunk.

If you answered yes to any three of these questions, you probably grew up money drunk.

If you answered yes to four or more of these questions, you can safely say you grew up money drunk.

# TWO

## TYPES OF
## MONEY
## DRUNKS

# CHAPTER 5

# THE
# COMPULSIVE
# SPENDER

Brilliant, highly, if not *over*educated, Ben is an easy man to like. Once a globetrotting traveler with an erudite religious tome to his credit, he remains a companionable conversationalist and, generally, what you might call a really nice guy—unless you were a merchant in his hometown.

Ben repeatedly buys things on sale to give himself a good shopping high and then returns them within 48 hours or so, after the buzz of the good deal is gone. Though they often are small, inexpensive, personal items such as watches, clothing, or tools, things that don't upset the salesclerks very much, Ben sometimes buys—and later returns—big-ticket items such as kitchen appliances, which aggravates the salesclerks a lot. This is not normal spending.

Since Ben is on a very small pension and strict budget, these items must go back to the store, and Ben prides himself on his ability to convince reluctant salesclerks of the fairness of his change of heart. The lure of the "sale" is impossible for Ben to ignore. Normal attempts to manage his money have not helped.

It is worth noting that for some money drunks the phrase "buying power" is quite literal. When the physical systems flood with stress, from strong emotions, negative or positive, we salve this physical distress by acting out in the money addiction. We, like Ben, must come to understand our spending as a compulsive act that covers up our fears and admit our powerlessness by seeking help.

## OUR NATIONAL EPIDEMIC

"When the going gets tough, the tough go shopping," a humorous lapel pin reads. For many money drunks this is no joke, as compulsive spending has become a national problem warranting extensive press coverage in recent times.

When stress hits compulsive spenders, we hit the stores. We relieve the anxiety in our lives with the high that spending produces in us.

After a fight with her husband or just before an important dinner party, Dorothy would go shopping and hide most of her purchases from her husband. Officially she'd be buying a new outfit because she suddenly had "nothing to wear." Of course, this was far from true.

"I had closets and closets full of clothes. It wasn't clothes I was after. It was power. When I felt powerless I would go shopping. I'd go to one of my favorite shops and touch everything. I would tell myself, 'I could buy this; I could have that.'"

As Dorothy sees it now, what she was trying to buy was a sense of control. The fights with her husband left her terrified. What if he abandoned her? Then who would she be? The important business parties left her frightened, too. What if they didn't like her? What if she disgraced her husband?

By shopping, Dorothy consoled her frightened inner child. She bought it something pretty the way a mother hands over a pacifier to a fussing infant. Instead of admitting her real fears, Dorothy focused on her stand-in fear. "I am afraid I will have nothing to wear" was just the bogus fear that blocked the real one: "I am afraid I am not lovable."

This fear keeps us chained to our compulsion. We say, "Just buy it," when we question a purchase. We have no patience, and we have no tolerance; not for others and certainly not for ourselves. "Charge it," we say, charging full steam ahead into debt. We often go one step beyond impulse buyers. We become compulsive buyers.

Hooked on shopping, Dorothy flooded her system with adrenaline like a hunter stalking big game. She strove desperately to ignore all the subtle symptoms and signals that were trying to tell her, "Danger! Stop, look, listen!" As much as any alcoholic woman who quietly drinks to combat loneliness, Dorothy's shopping was an attempt to medicate her moods. In the end, it didn't work and neither did her marriage. Her husband left with what remained of their money and Dorothy was forced to face her addiction alone.

Perhaps more than any other form of the money addiction, the need for compulsive spending is easily viewed as an attempt to block feelings of inadequacy and anxiety.

We're thinking here of Betty, a bright and bored housewife in her early forties. To her family and friends, she is a clear case of misdirected energy. To us, she is a Compulsive Spender, using her spending to block her feelings. College educated, a fine teacher back when she was a working professional, Betty has raised her children and lowered her expectations.

Although it would take less than a year to finish a graduate degree and allow herself to reenter the teaching arena at a nicely challenging level, she procrastinates over doing so, always citing "money" as her reason. (Her friends factor in "fear," but the money excuse keeps Betty from even looking at that.) Like the housewife who is a daily, closet drinker, Betty uses her spending to keep her distracted from her life. And she uses her sister's spending to distract her from her own.

Betty has three credit cards. ("Only three," she likes to say.) Her sister Jean has a dozen. For the last three years, two out of three of Betty's cards have stayed right at the limit, bumping their heads on her credit ceiling.

Because she only uses her "emergency card" and pays it like a monthly bill, Betty tells herself that she's doing well. Yet she doesn't have a savings account at all. "Every time that card gets clear it starts ticking," she complains. "It says, 'Buy something, do something, treat yourself to something,'" and Betty plays credit-card roulette.

What she tells herself, angrily, is that her new purchases prevent her from clearing up her old purchases. "But I'm doing okay," she rationalizes. "I'm not *really* using my cards."

She's right. Her cards are using her. By paying only the minimums on two of her cards, she pays her finance charge over and over—$500 due on one card, $2,000 due on another. "That's only twenty-five hundred dollars," she tells herself. At nearly 20 percent a year, it has cost her $1500 to maintain her card-carrying status these "no charge" years. (Do we need to tell you that $1500 is the cost of a semester's tuition at her university?)

The balance in our checkbook is not the only balance missing. Long accustomed to crisis management, we find a normal, balanced life very uncomfortable. We keep waiting for the shoe to drop, the creditor to call, the check to bounce. When disaster strikes, the furnace goes out, the car breaks down, an emergency root canal is needed, we Compulsive Spenders may breathe a little easier. This we understand. Crisis. As baffling as it may seem to the normal spender, we are actually more comfortable off balance than on. We are like sailors accustomed to walking the decks on stormy seas. Level ground feels foreign to us. We have grown comfortable with discomfort. Our money addiction has become an addiction to crisis.

For a Compulsive Spender, an emergency is an excuse, a carte blanche on further mismanagement. "I was doing okay until the car blew up," we tell ourselves. What we don't admit is that when the car blows up, we may binge spend our new savings account since "the car bill took such a bite out of it anyway."

The money addiction thrives on shame. It feeds our binges, whispering the terrible lie that we are not good enough because we don't have enough. "I can't afford it right now," a normal person might decide, contemplating an expensive purchase. To a Compulsive Spender, the same phrase is an indictment, a shameful confession of criminal guilt.

"I (lowly me, worthless me) cannot afford it (whatever 'it' is, luxury or not) right now because I'm too stupid, I should have more, I've mismanaged my funds, I've failed."

To a normal person, a shortage of ready cash is not the end of the world. To a Compulsive Spender, it starts the vicious cycle of low self-esteem that leads into the next big spending binge.

Without spending power, we feel truly powerless. A cash flow problem causes us to panic. Sure, we'd love to get our heads above water financially, but when you're trying to buy your self-worth the need for a short-term bit of esteem can overcome your best intentions to remain solvent. We buy now and promise to pay later and lose more and more self-worth. And go further and further into debt until, one day, we suddenly learn through bankruptcy, divorce, or poverty that we are at the end of our rope.

## THE WAY OUT

June is a recovering Compulsive Spender. A fragile, blue-eyed blonde with a powerhouse flair for business, June has every reason to have high self-esteem. She has pulled herself out of debt and begun a slow but steady climb toward solid success and corporate recognition. And yet, despite her bright future, June battles low self-worth and a chronic compulsion to overspend. As a practicing money drunk, she had battled it blindly for years, but in early financial recovery she began to see a pattern. (For June, as for many money drunks, abstinence had to precede clarity. She never knew why she overspent until she stopped doing it.) June's pattern of overspending was linked to feelings of humiliation. She overspent to overcompensate for what felt like slights.

"For me the need to spend money is linked to feelings of inferiority. This urge to buy is grounded in a basic sense of lack of power. It isn't things necessarily that I want to buy; I want to buy power. When they say 'buying power,' that to me is a very literal phrase."

In her first year of financial abstinence, June traveled abroad. All went well when she was in Germany, a country she found surprisingly genial and financially remunerative to her business concerns as well. She bought a few souvenirs, modest mugs and token cigarette lighters, but she had no real desire to overspend and buy everything with "Germany" stamped on it.

"This isn't so bad," June thought. Of course, neither was all the attention she was receiving as a visiting corporate star.

It was when she got to Britain that June felt her money-drunk syndrome begin to stir like a sleeping snake. She found England cold and chilly. Her business there went poorly. She couldn't seem to impress anyone with her talent or her product. She felt foolish, low, discouraged. She felt ill dressed, ill mannered, ill suited to the Continental life she had fantasized.

Sodden body and soul from the damp English weather and the dampened enthusiasm for her product, June suddenly fought an awakened compulsion to spend, needing constant prayer to avoid going into debt again.

As she recalls, "Traveling in England, I became aware not of a desire to acquire goods but a desire to feel good, by which I evidently meant competent. Disoriented by a foreign culture, constantly caught off guard in terms of social graces, I wanted to buy in order to compensate for my low opinion of myself."

In short, June wanted the quick fix to fix her feelings.

Because she had already hit bottom and did not want to hit another, lower, bottom, June was able to recognize that her urge to spend was actually an attempt to run from her feelings. She began carrying a small notebook with her in which she noted the circumstances in which her compulsion to spend arose. (Often, the mere acting of jotting down the desire served to defuse it.) Later that night, in the quiet and privacy of her bedroom, she would play detective to see what, exactly, had "set her off."

Because there is still so little consciousness around addictive spending, we have come to feel that keeping a journal (see Week Three of the 90-Day Program) is an invaluable tool for any recovering money drunk. We believe that an emotional journal is also a critical tool in unraveling the "why" behind the "what." June used her journal to maintain her abstinence and see a way out for herself.

Let us be clear that we do not believe that a Compulsive Spender must know *why* he or she overspends in order to stop doing it. As we have said, clarity often follows financial abstinence. We do, however, feel that any sustained recovery is greatly aided by the self-insight that keeping a journal provides.

Many Compulsive Spenders, rather than feel what we feel (which is often bad, small, flawed, stupid, invisible, foolish, a Failure), are often tempted to take the first "think." By this we mean that we slip back into grandiose thinking or into its twin, poverty thinking. Feeling out of control, we will very often attempt to gain a sense of control by either over- or underspending. This relapse begins in the mind, not in the pocket.

For a recovering Compulsive Spender, the first "think" can be as intoxicating as an alcoholic's first drink. That first, fatal sip of fantasy can lead us back to the intoxication of being money drunk. "If I just buy this, I'll feel great."

As Alan puts it: "I'm a compulsive spender. I've made a lot of money. I've lost a lot of money. For years my addictions kept me away from my family. My brother and sister were married to people I didn't know and had children I'd never met.

"In my first year of sobriety, traveling home to see them all for a Christmas holiday, it was very important for me to rent the big car (it was a Lincoln Continental) with a phone in it, even though I knew the phone wouldn't work in the mountains where they lived. I filled the trunk full of presents, appropriate to the occasion.

"I remember how hard it was to feel a part of the family after the presents had been opened. It was much easier to give the presents than to play with the children. I watched a lot of television.

"By the first year of my financial recovery several years later, I still had the grandiosity but not the cash to rent the car or buy the presents. I had been counting all my money and had made a money map but had not yet managed to save any money for presents. I made a decision just to skip going home for Christmas, as I'd skipped it all those years before sobriety.

"As I made plans for a quiet Christmas, my brother-in-law called to say he would give me a ride, that my family wanted to see me, that everyone wanted me to come home. I talked to my money buddy [see Week Seven of the 90-Day Program] about it and he said, 'Go.'

"My brother-in-law had a rattletrap car with no heater and a window taped shut. I didn't even like to be seen in it. I had no money for presents, but I went home.

"During the fourteen-hour car trip, I hit upon the idea of trying to teach my nieces and nephews something, as a present. I knew they were struggling with numbers. I decided to teach them to count to a hundred.

"I did. I was forced to share myself, my time. I sat them on my lap and for hours we went around and around . . . each taking a turn, one at a time . . . thirty-six, thirty-seven, thirty-eight, thirty-nine—thirty ten . . . no . . . forty!

"It took us three days. Last year's toys had been broken in three days. For the next two years, whenever they saw me or we talked on the phone, we *had* to count to a hundred . . .

"Sometimes now, years later, we still do."

For a Compulsive Spender on the way out, much of American advertising needs to be turned inside out. Bombarded with images that promise us self-worth with each new purchase, we must learn to earn our self-respect by riding out the waves of impulse that urge us to spend.

As we learn to weather stress without spending or debting to block our feelings, we learn that we have an unsuspected reservoir of inner strengths. Acknowledging this newly encountered strength, we understand for the first time that clothes do not make the man, character does. Instead of acting out in our own fantasy of the good life, we begin building character, a self we can be proud of.

## ARE YOU A COMPULSIVE SPENDER?

1. Do you buy things and hide them?

2. When you shop, do you get high and then crash?

3. Do you worry more about having money to spend than how to make it?

4. Do you play credit-card roulette, filling up one card and then moving to the next?

5. Do you impulsively buy things you don't need or can't afford?

6. Do you shop in order to alter your mood?

7. Do you rationalize useless purchases and extravagant gifts as "business"?

8. Do you find it impossible to stay within your budget or shopping list when you shop?

9. Do you continually drain your savings account or fail to have one?

10. Do you joke about your overflow of gadgets or accessories?

If you answered yes to any two of these questions, you may be a compulsive spender.

If you answered yes to any three of these questions, you are probably a compulsive spender.

If you answered yes to four or more of these questions, you can safely diagnose yourself as a compulsive spender.

# 6

## THE BIG DEAL
## CHASER

Ken is 33 years old, a former Green Beret, and father of two children. He has been married for 11 years. In January of 1991, he was managing a restaurant and living with his family in a nice three-bedroom home that they rented reasonably. He owned a car and a motorcycle, and some furniture. All of this sounds stable enough and would be—but Ken is a classic Big Deal Chaser. It only takes one deal, his latest, to show his entire pattern.

The Gulf War started and ended.

Ken saw the opportunity to "do something for the vets and make a few bucks, too." He thought a benefit concert and welcome-home parade would be terrific. After several calls he got a lot of interest and used his phone at work and at home to make arrangements, contacting the heads of many large companies as potential sponsors, even getting a letter from President Bush's office.

Ken called in favors from family and friends. He borrowed money from his father and asked for help writing the letters to sponsors. In short, he became addicted to the idea.

His wife was alternately impressed and disgusted, having seen this fire in his eyes before. There was the time he started a bodyguard service, a television stuntman company, a land development firm. Each of those new projects had left them broke again and near divorce. She tried to be supportive but when she questioned him about their dwindling finances Ken became angry and threw tantrums, which is typical Big Deal Chaser behavior. The anger is a sign of Ken's insecurity.

Within a month Ken lost his restaurant job. He didn't need it anyway, he thought; he was going to pull this one off. He didn't tell his brothers he had lost the job until after he had borrowed money for his phone bill. Weeks later, in desperation, he took out loans on the car and motorcycle. Within three months they were both gone, repossessed by some unpatriotic bank officer who didn't understand what a wonderful thing Ken was doing.

Slowly realizing that hundreds of people had called armed forces bases with the same idea and that many professional concert promoters were holding concerts all over America, he was evicted from the lovely home and his wife packed the kids and herself off to live somewhere far away from Ken.

It is hard for Ken to see that he has done this same thing over and over again. Each of his big deals has had its own siren's call and reasons that it couldn't fail.

Like the drinker who drinks to *escape* problems but whose drinking *causes* problems, Big Deal Chasers don't see the big deal as our problem but as our solution. So pervasive is this belief that it often shapes our whole personal identity—an identity based in grandiosity. Just as the Compulsive Spender believes that his great new purchase will alter his life for the better, the Big Deal Chaser fantasizes an outsized future in which he is free from normal human concerns, such as insecurity and pain.

The Big Deal Chaser espouses, in our opinion, one of the most difficult belief systems to change. Masquerading as ambition, it is, in fact, something far more pernicious and soul destroying. It is an addiction to revenge: "I'll show them. I'll make so much money they'll have to respect me." In the minds of Big Deal Chasers money will fix everything. Our parents will love us. Our children will show us off. Our spouses will look at us with new ardor.

Once the big deal is signed, we'll have a pocketful of hundreds, never have to ask a price, feel like the person we really are. Flashing those hundreds like a passkey, we'll have access. We'll get what we want. Money is power and power is the ultimate aphrodisiac.

And what is a big deal?

It is the sudden change that changes everything else.

It's the big idea that will make us rich, the new great job that will pay us five times the money. It's the new invention. It's the big sale, the new client, the inside straight, the hot tip. It's the long shot, the movie sale, the thing that will make us millions. It's the lottery.

It's why we work late, committing the "overtime crime" and leaving our life to be lived when we have it made. It's the magic number, the $20,000, the $200,000, the $2,000,000 that we need to set everything right. It's the business promiscuity that keeps us working on side deals at the boss's expense. It's a cold-cash femme fatale that lures us, leads us on, leads us away from our job, our family, our daily responsibilities.

## THE MAGIC NUMBER

All Big Deal Chasers like fairy tales. We like the pot of gold at the end of the rainbow; we like the Midas touch. Memories of Donald Trump in Trump Towers with his lavish yacht and his Georgia peach girlfriend and his showy Nordic wife offer a vision of opulence that we may alter, tastefully, in our imaginations but that still has a significant appeal for some.

Most Big Deal Chasers don't feel we really need a billion—although it would be nice—but many do have what we call "a magic number," an amount that would make everything all right—if we had it.

Patrick had always wished for a job where he made $40,000 a year, his magic number. He got it. Then he wished for a job where he made $100,000 a year, his next magic number. He got that, too. He remembers the day he showed his friends the commission check for $175,000, the day he showed them his new BMW, the day he showed them *both* of his new high-rise apartments: one for work, one for pleasure.

What Patrick does not remember is his friends begging, "Patrick, save some of this money. Buy yourself a home. Take a reasonable salary for yourself and bank the rest of it. *Don't spend it all. . . .*"

What Patrick did not tell them was that he already had a new magic number: one million. He thought about it constantly. He had to have it. Then he would finally *feel* successful. Then he would invest sensibly, slow down, improve the quality of his life by taking time for his friends and his intellectual interests.

When he had a million, he would feel like a million, Patrick knew. What he didn't know was the magic had stopped working.

Expecting special treatment when it came to his financial obligations, Patrick borrowed for his high-rise rents, and begged his creditors for more time. The borrowing made him feel like a lowlife. He tapped his friends, sure that the magic would return and they'd all make a killing. But all that died was their faith in Patrick's magic.

Alone in a restaurant, he told himself he was still okay, still credible, still "magic." He only needed $150,000 to get out of debt. Why, he'd made that much in a year. Of course, he'd spent it all, but . . . Aiming for $200,000, Patrick borrowed a little more, just to tide him over one last time, just because. . . .

Because Patrick had to lose everything: his apartments, his car, his job, his friends. He had to stand alone at his high-rise window and watch as his self-image came crashing down. In that moment, the only magic number Patrick fixed on was the number of floors to his death: floors in the air versus seconds in the air.

For a money drunk like Patrick, hitting bottom is a dangerous thing. Patrick was lucky. He didn't jump. Months earlier, one of his high-roller friends had found his way toward solvency. Grateful just to be alive, Patrick followed.

Patrick's new magic number became zero. He wanted zero owed on credit cards. Zero owed to friends. Zero owed in back rent.

## THE OVERTIME CRIME: WORKAHOLISM

Not all money drunks who chase the big deal do so on a scale that is so obvious. For many, the big deal is pursued through the slower, more subtle, and equally deadly pursuit of workaholism. The big deal for these money drunks translates to "enough" salary and "enough" recognition in the workplace to salve their low self-esteem.

In talking with workaholics, a chord that we found struck repeatedly was "instant amnesia" about their accomplishments. The analogy we found ourselves using was that every day they went to "life school" and wrote their names and good deeds on the blackboard and every night their low self-worth sneaked in and erased their good record.

No matter how much they had done to prove themselves worthy, the proof never seemed to tilt the scales in their favor.

Always behind, they were always playing catch-up—and they never quite could.

When we met Betty we found her highly personable—and highly driven. By any reasonable standard, she had long since become successful. What we learned in working with her was that reason had nothing to do with the impossible standards she set for herself.

Because a fixation with money is something that most people keep to themselves, or try to, many money drunks pass for normal, hardworking people. When we first heard Betty describe herself this way and then mention in passing a seventy-five-hour work week, we wondered, "Normal to whom?"

Betty is a lawyer, 41 years old. She has worked all of her life. Her work has brought her some real accomplishments, but not enough to please Betty, or her family. Reared to be an over-achiever, Betty achieves over and over, taking no satisfaction in any small victory. She refuses to take vacations, feeling that she cannot afford to. She stays focused on the future day when the victory will be big enough, the money substantial enough, that all the years of self-hate, self-doubt, self-deprivation will suddenly be balanced out.

Underneath her frantic pursuit of bigger, grander clients, Betty is afraid of looking foolish, looking lonely; afraid of looking at herself at all. And so, she focuses her attention on the glorious future, the someday when she will be somebody important and somebody will have to love her for it, while her friends and family tease her about the amount of time she spends at work.

For Betty the big deal equals love and respect. The big deal equals a personal warranty that her life has been worthwhile, not misspent, not foolish.

What Betty doesn't know is that for all money drunks, the big deal, the future, the final payoff never happens. Even the most noble causes are pursued one day at a time.

While other people need to learn to love themselves, Betty

seeks to be loved by others, to be an exception. By working constantly, she believes she'll finally be a big deal herself.

But that's not how life works. External approval is a fantasy, and many workaholics don't hit bottom until they get too physically sick to carry on any longer. As the old saying goes, "No one looks back on their life and wishes they had spent more time at the office."


## SELF-ESTEEM: THE REALLY BIG DEAL

It is a paradox of financial recovery that self-worth, self-respect, and self-esteem must *precede* success—not follow it.

We often believe we are what we earn. We are what we own. We are *what we owe*. The idea that we could count for something all on our own is foreign to us.

Besides keeping a running tally on what each of our friends has banked, a personal game of who's on first, who's on second, we know which professional ballplayers get what. How much each star gets paid for each big film. Reading the news, we gravitate toward rags-to-riches stories. We may become depressed at being a "have-not" because we are obsessed with those who "have."

Big Deal Chasers are often brilliant and intuitive and may have sensed at an early age the difference between the haves and the have-nots. The addictive struggle to rise above our station and make a mark is fueled by the same resentment that may fuel the outlaws among us who mistakenly hunt ways to make it out of poverty through such illegal means as drug dealing, prostitution, embezzlement, swindling, or gambling. This may be the natural progression of the money disease in its advanced stages.

Sam is a recovering artist, 12 years sober off alcohol and drugs. When he entered treatment, he admitted to himself he was addicted to alcohol and drugs.

Sam now believes his first addiction was to cash. Money gave Sam a high he never matched elsewhere. The drugs and alcohol numbed his feelings until he could find a way to make some "good money."

For Sam, that way turned out to be dealing. Buying and selling drugs gave him access to free drugs and easy money. As his addiction progressed, so did his need for money, but Sam says, "I wasn't the kind of addict that only dealt to feed my drug habit. I dealt because my habit was ready cash."

Sam remembers his rationale. "Back in 1970, it was just like the old rum-running. We always said to ourselves, 'The Kennedys did it—that's how they built their fortune,'" (referring to Joseph Kennedy's alleged bootlegging activities).

From a little light dealing among friends, Sam progressed to involvement with some international smugglers.

"One flight from the Bahamas with a few bales of pot, and presto, thousands of dollars in cash. In my pocket." Sam still savors the thought, as for a sober alcoholic, the "taste" remains.

Sam continues, "I realize that it was the pocket full of cash, the *I am somebody* power of it, the *right now, baby* immediacy that led me further and further down the road. From an ounce of grass here and there in college, to dealing with forklifts down in Miami with guys who counted their money by weighing it."

Only half-jokingly, Sam says, "It was the twenty thousand dollars down my boot that made the habit literally hard to kick."

For Sam, as for many of us, his addictions intertwined. Alcohol, drugs, money, and sex were all part of the potent cocktail he downed.

Sam continues, "Being a money drunk gave me contempt for myself, and for women." As he explains, "There was always a girl or two who was as addicted to money as I was, and we had a lot of fun as long as the money held up."

In recovery, Sam kicked alcohol, drugs, and addictive sex

long before he looked at his money addiction. Even sober, he was able to sell himself the premise that his lust for cash was really the American Dream.

"Years after I was detoxed from the substance abuse, I was still trying to come down from the money addiction. I had been small change in the big picture of illegal business, but I tasted enough to get hooked. Cash was king."

Sam still feels the calling of the physical high that high rolling afforded him. It was a rush through his whole system.

"I think the money rush is the same high-octane excitement that fuels almost all illegal endeavors, whether bootlegging, robbery, manipulative stock trading, embezzlement, or even many legal ones like gambling. They can all become addictive because the payoff is exactly that, a *payoff.*"

"Everyone has his price," Sam told himself before sobriety. In recovery, he was told such feelings were cynical and ill founded; still, it took a long time in therapy and many years of prayer before his cynicism began to lift. Before his obsession with money (and the power he believed it provided) was lifted, he came to understand that money was only a temporary fix for his low self-worth and that illegal money was a house of cards.

"When I first got sober I had no self-esteem because I had not done any estimable things," observes Sam. "No matter how much cash I had, often with a limousine driver, and a boat on the bay, it was never enough. It took years of recovery and service work to build a *me* I can be proud of."

It is also our experience that once a Big Deal Chaser (or any money drunk) finds solvency, we begin to express whatever moral outrage we may have at the inequalities in the world in positive and direct ways such as volunteer work, donations, and political activism. These expressions of conscience, we believe, are the constructively directed anger of the Big Deal Chaser that formerly fed the driving need to succeed at any cost.

## BOTTOMING OUT

For the Big Deal Chaser, the bottom often begins with a sense of hollowness. There is a feeling of, "I've been here before," when we hear ourself winding up for the big sales pitch.

We're talking condos in Hawaii and open our mail to find a birth announcement from our college roommate with a note saying the family is fine. Suddenly, the swinging singles condo begins to sound a little shabby. Despite ourselves, normal begins to sound, well, normal. Even attractive.

Julian, a software designer, grew up in the suburbs, got to the big city at 20, and stayed there chasing blondes and business deals for another 20 years. Hooked on the big deal, he chased high-rise jacuzzis and high-roller friends.

"The suburbs make me hyperventilate," Julian always joked to his friends. "So much grass. So many families."

When his last big deal hit bottom, Julian went into a depression so bad that he took to the suburbs to stay for a week with his brother. "Birds, trees, children . . . the full catastrophe," he moaned on returning. "It was Uncle Julian this, Uncle Julian that."

In short, Julian was called "Uncle Julian" often enough that he finally thought about really being one. What would it be like, he wondered, to just live in the now? Without the big deal to define him, Julian had to ask the big question, "Who am I?"

Big Deal Chasers often believe—falsely—that if we get enough money and have enough things we will gain enough approval to satisfy our longing for it. And so, we pursue money as a shortcut to self-worth.

We have found that most money drunks think that what we want is money when it is actually acceptance that we are after.

"I'm working on this big development," a Big Deal Chaser

likes to be able to say. We do not want to talk about putting in an ordinary day's work because we do not want to feel like an ordinary guy, a "worker among workers." When he resolved to try being one, Julian's financial picture changed immediately.

## THE WAY OUT

For the Big Deal Chaser on the way out from the magic number, financial health involves a willingness to focus on the *now*.

Patrick recently got the $200,000 he was hoping and working for. But this time Patrick had been working on the first steps of financial solvency. He had already moved into inexpensive housing. He had gotten a job that paid him weekly and he made his commitments to it first, leaving his other speculative work for his off hours. He made the paycheck job his number-one priority and he paid his bills and stopped the debting spiral. He got used to a moderate lifestyle based on his pay and not his wish for big money. In short, he didn't need the money. He was already living the life he wanted to be living.

So this time Patrick is changing little about his lifestyle. He used the Windfall Rule from Week Eight of the 90-Day Program and paid a third to the past (debts), a third to the present (reward), and a third to the future (savings). *After* he paid his taxes. His financial solvency has taught him two critical things: One, that every deal is just one deal in a continuing body of work, so he stopped waiting to live his life; and two, that self-esteem is an inside job, so he no longer needs to broadcast his success.

At root, an addiction to a magic number is an addiction to emotional procrastination. "When I have the magic number, *then* . . ." we tell ourselves. *Then* we will be happy, satisfied, fulfilled. In solvency, the waiting has got to go. The "When I get it, then I'll be happy" aspect of our personalities, which has always kept us postponing happiness and postponing satisfaction, must bite the dust.

It is said, endlessly, that all spiritual growth is "an inside job." Unfortunately, this tiresome phrase is dead accurate. For the magic number to be eradicated, we must make a firm inner resolve that whatever we have and are, right now, is "enough."

For a money drunk recovering from the magic number, it is necessary to come off the high horse, to stop living like the money is in hand, to get a handle on finances as they stand, right now.

How much money is there really? The Counting and Money Maps that we do in the program section give us immediate clarity about the real status of our finances, and take much of the worry out of the process.

With the big deal gone, living day to day becomes the issue. No more fancy restaurants if we can't afford them. It's time to buy groceries. Time to pay rent. Time to go to work, even for someone else. Even a job where we may have to punch in and out.

Life comes to scale. We become life-size, but so do our problems. For someone recovering from the big deal, this is a new experience.

Often, this "life-size" life requires an immediate reduction in living standards. The high-rent apartment, the expensive car (if either are even left) may give way to other things more within our means. When they do, the temptation is to find a "quick fix," another deal to chase away our feelings of inadequacy, of vulnerability, of loss. What we are really doing is coming back into reality.

Working with newly recovering money drunks, we find it necessary to remind them repeatedly that they are involved in a classic grieving process. The newly money-sober Big Deal Chaser is really grieving an image of self, the self who was larger than life, the self who was immune to life's problems. And this feels like dying. We mourn that self-image that was so outsized it was large enough to cover our gaping flaws. We will miss this super-self. Without it, we may feel too small, too fragile, too vulnerable.

Sometimes, we may believe our newly experienced feelings will overwhelm us, even kill us. In Mark's early financial sobriety, his panic attacks caused him many sleepless nights. And Julia remembers repeating over and over, "I don't know who I am."

"I can't stand it!" she would wail. "I'm invisible. I'm going to end up a bag lady." These were terrible feelings that she was going through, but they were not facts about her future, non-addicted life. She had to remind herself: feelings will pass.

Rather than stop, look, and listen for what the universe has in store for us, we may leap at the first "big deal opportunity." We take one more hotshot sales job we hate. We may make one more grab for the brass ring we don't really even want.

Julia recalls working with a woman who "had" to have a big deal job right away. The job she chose? One with an active alcoholic who was addicted to pain pills and to compulsive lying. Although her friends urged her to keep looking until something sane showed up, this was "not an option," in her words. Blinded by the promise of quick money as a quick fix for her discomfort, she had to take the job. Two months later her boss was in detox, her job was over, and she was back on the street with less cash than before.

To recover from all big deal chasing, a money drunk (male or female) must learn to stand still and pause long enough to get quiet and ask: "What do I really need?" This is the question we never really ask. We *think* we already know the answer. What we think we need is money. Lots of money. Taking our first steps toward financial sobriety, we soon learn that that isn't true.

What we really want is self-respect. What we really want is recognition from our peers. For this, we don't need money. Honesty is the stock in trade that friendships bank on. And, when we are honest with ourselves, it is *love* that we are after. We just thought we could buy it.

Oh, come on . . . *love*?

Money drunks are skeptics and we often catch ourselves sneering, "Love is not going to pay my rent."

Loving ourselves means treating ourselves with dignity; and a rent so high we cannot pay it without mortgaging our souls is not a price worth paying any longer.

Don't get us wrong. We definitely *are* in favor of "bettering" ourselves. We believe strongly in constructive change and positive personal growth. Mark worked full-time while he went to high school, college, and graduate school at night, and Julia has always worked full-time as a teacher and writer even while being a single mother.

We definitely believe in working toward a worthy dream. What is college, for example, but a long-term investment in our futures? We *are* saying that a money drunk can no longer speculate on a "long shot" future at the cost of the present day. As actors say, "Don't quit your day job."

There is a difference between appropriate speculation and chasing the big deal, and that difference is often lost on money drunks.

The difference is this: When we are chasing the big deal, we count on the money from it to pay our bills. We become convinced that our deal is going to be so big and make so much money that we can justify borrowing from family, friends, our spouses' savings, anything. And if the big deal doesn't happen, which they often don't, we lose everything, or close to it.

When we are *not* chasing the big deal, we keep our bills up-to-date and don't borrow money from anyone to pay our expenses. We work extra hours on our own time and expense to pursue that great opportunity, whatever it might be.

The nights at college or the extra free-lance job as we save toward a home—these are a respected part of life, a healthy way to express our ambitions. The early morning stolen hours at a desk while we pen our first book, the extra hours worked while saving for a new car are a few of the many ways we can (and do) better our lot in life. These long-term investments in ourselves bear small resemblance to the fast-money schemes a Big Deal Chaser banks on.

On our way out, we learn how to risk intelligently, how to move out in faith without needing to move in on the charity of friends, family, and spouse. Successful entrepreneurs take moderate risks. That phrase, "Don't quit your day job," is good advice. It means keep a roof over your head. It means: "Don't borrow from friends because you will lose them."

By "living in the now," paying rents we can afford, paying as we go instead of borrowing against our futures, recovering Big Deal Chasers purchase self-love that enables us to shape a future that we want instead of one we think we have to have.

When Mark surrendered the big deal fix, he began to find himself. He became more involved with his family, was able to get married, began to write his first fiction in many years, and even taught in Russia as a guest of the Academy of Science. In short, he began to build a solid good character. And good character is a prized possession that no one can ever take away.

Humility is not the same thing as humble pie. What we have not been able to absorb into our systems is the idea of real humility—being one worker among many, one friend among a body of friends.

Most Big Deal Chasers have lost all touch with the concept of being of service. We want to be stars. Although we often tell ourselves differently, the truth is that a great deal of our overtime work is grounded in wanting to be heroic. If somebody has to "save the day," we want it to be us. This is a noble sentiment that does not work in the long run, because it is hard to combine low self-worth with a need for a high profile.

In financial sobriety, this attitude has to change. Oddly, when it does, we are often far more successful than we ever were in our money-drunk days. This is because we have finally surrendered and become more focused.

Chasing the big deal, we used our business promiscuity to avoid committing to the project at hand, although it greatly sabotaged our chances for any substantial and long-term business success. Most of us found it was a two-headed problem. With our big deal chasing we always focused on the future, while our business promiscuity caused us to indulge in constantly scanning the horizon for alternate projects and new get rich quick schemes.

All commitment has a "single-pointed" quality. Early in recovery many Big Deal Chasers have a hard time focusing on one area that interests them. Our business promiscuity has left us dazzled and confused by the array of possibilities. In trying to be single-pointed, we do best to focus on the spiritual concept of service. In that, at least, we can be well focused, bringing our minds back to the principle of service whenever it wants to romance another new option instead.

"Helping God's kids get done what they think they need to get done," is the way the late Gayle W., a successful Los Angeles real estate entrepreneur, gave her recipe for success. A Louisville, Kentucky, girl who went from being a flight attendant to being a millionaire, she credited her financial rewards to her willingness to work for others. Rather than try to sell a buyer a home, any home, she tried to sell them the home they actually would be happy in. In other words, work for a common goal, not personal aggrandizement.

To a practicing Big Deal Chaser, such altruism sounds hopelessly idealistic. After all, business is business. And yet, if Ken had remembered this recovery recipe, he might not have lost everything. He would have stayed focused on his day job and not risked everything. He forgot that "Easy Does It" means: Easy Accomplishes It.

On the way out of big deal chasing, one must learn that the phrase "Easy Does It" is not just some bromide, meaning "calm down." Used, instead, as a modus operandi, a mode of business conduct, the phrase tells us that a slow, balanced approach accomplishes far more substantial gains in the long run than the old, self-willed "power blitzes" ever did. The way out means balance.

In recovering from workaholism, the overtime crime, Big Deal Chasers must move toward center. We must allow ourselves to be human, not superhuman, drop our impossible demands on others to perceive us as heroic, and drop our impossible demands on ourselves to *be* heroic. Instead of trying to save the day, we focus on saving ourselves.

Saving ourselves means saving a part of each day for self-nurturance: a twenty-minute walk home through the park, a quiet lunch break with a sandwich and a bookstore visit instead of a power-driven lunch with clients or with work at our desk. Instead of doing the same old thing, we do something else. We slow down.

Betty used the Time Grid from Week Ten of the 90-Day Program to establish playtime for herself in every day and to schedule time for her family just as she would a business meeting. This schedule included "free time" in which she allowed herself to do whatever she wanted. This was very difficult at first.

Accustomed to overwork, we are also accustomed to underplay. Play is something many workaholics need to learn to do.

"The imagination at play" is not an empty phrase. Many of us have learned that by allowing ourselves the luxury of play, we actually work far better. Turning to our tasks refreshed, we often find new solutions to old problems.

In recovering from workaholism, we Big Deal Chasers stop making our jobs the sole focus for our self-worth. We actively seek recreational activities in which we re-create ourselves into more balanced beings.

Instead of leaching our spiritual nutrients dry, we begin to replenish our supply. We seek out classes in adult education, books on "crazy" topics that interest us, new crafts that expand our skills and our souls.

No longer our only calling card, jobs become something we do (and probably do better), not something we are. No longer required to bear the whole burden of our identities, jobs may even change. The "high prestige" job that doesn't suit us may be abandoned for the more rewarding but lower-profile one. Alternatively, those of us working in jobs far below our skill levels find ourselves becoming more confident about a change toward work more in line with our level of competency. We begin to feel more confident as we become more solvent.

## ARE YOU A BIG DEAL CHASER?

1. Do you (even secretly) think the world owes you a living?

2. Do you have angry mood swings if your schemes are questioned?

3. Does it cost you more to live than you make?

4. Do you expect special treatment and special understanding when you cannot meet your financial commitments?

5. Do you start strong and finish weak when your big deal pans out smaller than you hoped for?

6. Does your lucky break have to be "sudden" and "huge" and "impressive"?

7. Do you refuse to watch your money since the big deal is going to make everything all right?

8. Do you have a "magic number," and has it gone up?

9. Do you spend the big deal before you sign it?

10. Do friends, family, or co-workers tease you about the amount of time you spend at work?

If you answered yes to any two of these questions, you may be a Big Deal Chaser.

If you answered yes to any three of these questions, you are probably a Big Deal Chaser.

If you answered yes to four or more of these questions, you can safely diagnose yourself as a Big Deal Chaser.

# CHAPTER

# 7

## THE
## MAINTENANCE
## MONEY DRUNK

Dana is a car salesman. His father was a car salesman, and Dana followed in Dad's footsteps. "I started hanging around the car lots when I was about eleven to be with Dad because he worked all the time. I would wash cars and sort of hang out. Then when I got old enough I delivered cars and ran errands and soon I was selling. It just happened that way."

Dana's father died two years ago, and Dana grieved not only for his father but for his own 20 years in the car business as well. "I realized I always hated this business but I didn't know how to make money any other way. I had never done anything that I felt was my own dream of what to do with my life."

The Maintenance Money Drunk is the most subtle of the money drunk types and therefore the most difficult to detect. It differs from the workaholic in that there is no red flag of flagrant behavioral dysfunction. The workaholic draws attention to his or her illness by chronic absenteeism from family and friends. The Maintenance Money Drunk, on the other hand, is physically present but psychologically absent, growing bitter or numb from the inability to pursue or even name his or her dreams.

Maintenance Money Drunks do not appear drunk on money. We are like the quiet alcoholic drinkers who drink to maintain. Never conspicuously drunk or out of control, we are never really sober, either. Our lives are lives of quiet desperation, never really knowing what *our* dreams are, or having too little faith to pursue them, or of knowing them all too well and not being able to risk our security to pursue them. Often semi-depressed, we use our money to medicate our discontent, rather than asking what might make us really happy.

Frank is a Maintenance Money Drunk. The life he's led is not his own. We tell his story because it shows so clearly the intertwining of the corrupted American Dream (the dream that used to be about freedom and justice) and the money addiction.

Ever since he was a little boy, Frank dreamed of being a writer. "Who taught you to write like this?" he remembers his high school teacher, Miss Price, exclaiming with delight. Frank cherished the compliment. Good writing meant a lot to him. *His* writing meant a lot to him. His family thought his writing was not practical.

Like Miss Price, Frank believed that his writing mattered terribly and that he had the talent to do it. He knew he could write, that he was meant to write, that writing was what he loved and what would give his life meaning. The only thing that came even a distant second was music, so maybe, he thought, he would write some songs, too.

And maybe he would have. His money addiction (and his family's money addiction) got in the way because for them money was everything.

"To my family, the arts just weren't practical," Frank recalls. "My father wanted me to run a bank. Any job that paid a lot was the right job in his eyes. To him, writing seemed just too risky."

A man who had buried his own dreams to support his family, Frank's father did not encourage large dreams in his sons. He himself felt financially unstable. A hard worker married to a compulsive-shopper wife, he found that no amount of work ever seemed to tally up to enough to cover her appetite for new and needless purchases.

Embittered by this himself, he urged his sons toward career paths more lucrative than his own. Yes, he wanted them to go to college, but he thought business college might be the right choice. Frank and his brothers took this advice to heart. They had to because it was hammered into them. Money makes the man, Frank's father preached.

And so, pressured by financial insecurity and the family belief that money was all that mattered, Frank abandoned his dream. For years, he worked to bring home the paycheck and talked about how "someday" he would write. "When I have enough money. . . ."

Somehow, no matter how much money Frank did make, there was never enough to buy the thing he wanted most, the freedom to be a writer. While Poverty Addicts (see Chapter Eight) might forgo following their dream because of a lack of money, Maintenance Money Drunks forgo following their dream because of a lack of time. Earning addictively, Frank became so caught up in his pursuit of material possessions that he ricocheted from one financial career choice to another, always feeling that his real life would start as soon as he could afford the time. Whereas the Big Deal Chaser believes that life begins when the deal comes through, the Maintenance Money Drunk believes that life is already over and the die is cast. He is doing what he must do and has no choice. Powerless, he can only medicate his despair with chronic dreaming. He is the Walter Mitty of the money world. Finally, in his mid-thirties, unhappy with all of his choices, Frank suffered a bankruptcy that left him penniless despite all his hard work; busted and broken, he finally let himself write.

By day, Frank pounded nails as a carpenter's helper. By night, he pounded away at the typewriter. Physically exhausted but spiritually exhilarated, Frank found his life had a curious balance to it. He felt like a failure by his family's terms but a success for the first time in terms of his own dreams.

## WISHING AND HOPING

As Maintenance Money Drunks, our lives are often shaped by people and forces outside ourselves, by our family's expectations, or by cultural mores instead of personal ones. This means that we will often pursue money and money-related stature without questioning why we are engaged in such a pursuit.

For the Maintenance Money Drunk, the pursuit of happiness has become the pursuit of the Almighty Dollar. Salaries are our gods and our goals. We do not ask, "Do I love my work?" We ask, "What does it pay?" If it pays regularly enough, we seldom think the cost of such living is too high. Unlike the Big Deal Chaser, we are always ready to settle.

Like many other Americans, Maintenance Money Drunks have forgotten what the American Dream really was. We have been confused by our society's focus on materialism. We have lost sight of our dream's true meaning, that of freedom and dignity.

Jack, 40, is a waiter at one of the best restaurants in Chicago. He has had restaurant jobs since he got his psychology degree from Michigan State in 1972. Since then he has read every book on psychology that has been published, and he regularly reads several human potential magazines a week. He tells his friends he is going to be a counselor but the cash-money restaurant business and the late night lifestyle keep him stuck.

One of the telltale symptoms of the Maintenance Money Drunk is the phrase "I'm going to," heard over and over again without action toward the goal. We often say that the greatest gift of solvency is learning how to turn a wish into a goal. And action is the difference between someone who is really going to do something and someone who is just wishing.

"I'm going to write a book." So write one page a day.

"I'm going back to school." So call the local college.

"I'm going to be an actor." So take a monologue class.

It is the concrete action, however small, that moves us out of maintaining our status quo and heads us toward our stated dreams and goals. The Maintenance Money Drunk medicates instead.

Unlike the Big Deal Chaser who is always acting on a specific scheme, the lie of the Maintenance Money Drunk is that "next year," we will do something about this stupid job, next year we will set about realizing a dream, next year we will spend more time with the kids.

Sometimes we have been lying to ourselves so long about doing something "later" that we begin to lose faith in our abilities. Then we stay where we are out of fear. And we begin to hate ourselves for it. We use money and our jobs to cover for our own feelings of loss and helplessness and boredom.

We must understand: The clock on our life is already ticking. It's game day.

## THE WAY OUT

For the Maintenance Money Drunk, recovery may begin with a period of rebellion. Remember the famous scene in the film *Network* where the citizens raised their windows to shout into the streets their anthem, "I'm mad as hell and I'm not going to take it anymore"? Maintenance money drunks are usually mad as hell as soon as they realize that the life they have been wasting is their own.

"I'm mad as hell and I'm not going to chase it anymore!" is the way one recovering Maintenance Money Drunk phrases it. "It" is the twisted American Dream. We must learn that all work is to be valued and value our own desires enough to pursue them. Now.

For many of us, getting solvent is a process of retrieval. We begin to retrieve our energy from the many other people and agendas we have invested in and draw that same energy back into our own core where we can begin to use it as we see fit.

Viewed in these terms, the withdrawal from maintenance money addiction is less a process of having something (our procrastination) removed from us and more a matter of our removing *ourselves* from people and situations that do not really serve our true interests.

For many Maintenance Money Drunks, life was always being postponed "until . . ." On the way out, we stop postponing our interests and our dreams. One day at a time, we take small steps in the directions that interest us. We begin to do more of what we love, not just what we should.

This process of giving ourselves permission to live our own lives, not the lives we have been programmed to lead, can release an enormous amount of energy. Many of us have suffered from a low-grade depression, and, as it begins to lift, we feel the rage we were masking with our despair. That rage feels scary. We need to remember that we can use it as fuel.

We are angry. And we have a right to be angry. We have frittered away our lives and our dreams and now we want to play catch-up. And that is exactly what we must learn to do, in small, regular doses. We must learn to channel our anger into actions on our own behalf.

It is very difficult for us to recognize and nurture our true selves. It's a lot easier to buy a Walkman than it is for most of us to simply take a walk. It is easier to run away into a movie or a television show than it is to go running. The most important way to learn how to exercise our options is to exercise, period. Unlike Big Deal Chasers, Maintenance Money Drunks must shift from passivity to action. Actions centering on self-care such as exercise are the place to begin.

In recovering from a life of money maintenance misery, there are two doses of medicine that, when taken regularly, even for a period of only 90 days, begin to effect strong and deep changes in our lives.

The first change is that we must exercise our bodies. Though this is true for all money drunks it is especially true for the Maintenance Money Drunks who may have taken to a sedentary lifestyle, hiding in television, for instance, in order to tune out the sound of the neglected dreams making all that racket in our heads. We have found that walking is an ideal way to begin the clearing process that changing long-ingrained life patterns entails. A brisk, daily 20-minute walk, longer if possible, functions on two levels:

Spiritually, a walk leaves us refreshed and renewed. Even in the city, we find areas of beauty to focus on: the window box gardens, the man with the matching dog, the elaborate cornice five stories up we never noticed before.

Physically, a walk rebalances our adrenaline level, which means that our stresses are lowered. Many of us have found that exercise is the difference between bearable stress and unbearable tension, and it also gives us time to think.

Secondly, we must exercise our dreams. As Maintenance Money Drunks, most of us have buried a dream. In recovery, we begin to gently unearth it. A beginning acting class in a church basement. A martial arts class. A needlework circle. Anything that gets us out of the house. Our choices have varied widely but the one common denominator is that what they offer us is joy. In recovery we must stop discounting our interests as being grandiose or beyond us. If the Big Deal Chaser must come down to size, the Maintenance Money Drunk must take a full breath and grow to size.

Part of the progression toward financial sobriety is gaining a sense of dignity for any job well done and beginning to evaluate ourselves on broader criteria than just money; for instance, how we parent our children, care for our extended families, participate in community actions and politics; in short, live as good citizens.

As recovering Maintenance Money Drunks, we need to do at least one thing daily that makes us happy. Because above all recovery should look like fun. It is.

## ARE YOU A MAINTENANCE MONEY DRUNK?

1. Is the pay the only thing you like about your job?

2. Does your work conflict with your value system?

3. Do you make "home improvements," instead of "life improvements?"

4. Have you cheated yourself of money in your budget for entertainment? (self-enrichment?)

5. Do you feel stuck?

6. Do you frequently abort plans for new projects?

7. Do you often complain about what you might have been?

8. Have you lost respect for yourself?

9. Have you become apathetic?

10. Does this line of questioning make you sad?

If you answered yes to any two of these questions, you may be a Maintenance Money Drunk.

If you answered yes to any three of these questions, you probably are a Maintenance Money Drunk.

If you answered yes to four or more of these questions, you can safely diagnose yourself as a Maintenance Money Drunk.

# CHAPTER
# 8

## THE POVERTY ADDICT

Julia was a well-known teacher and writer teaching graduate-level courses at the finest universities, where her students revered her. Her articles appeared in some of the best publications in the country. She was even, in some circles, famous. She had written for network television and movie studios and even made a feature film; yet, after 20 years of a well-publicized career, she had no savings and lived in a tiny rental house, driving a car that didn't start when it rained.

Looking into her past, this is understandable.

Julia's mother kept a beautiful house and her father always made good money and provided well, but Julia's mother was so frugal she often went without. No fancy clothes for her, "just good sense."

Julia recalls, as a little girl, wanting her mother to be happy. "I used to buy her pretty blue glass beads from Woolworth's as a treat, but she never wore them. When I was older, I saved all of my money to buy her a brightly colored blouse but she never wore that either. She had one beautiful wool suit, a deep teal blue. She said she 'had to have it' for my father's business outings as though it were not okay to have bought a pretty thing just for her."

Julia grimaces. "I went through high school with four skirts, two Catholic plaid ones and two corduroy skirts I had made myself."

Like any other teenage girl, Julia longed for pretty clothes and some girlish frou-frou. She wasn't allowed it. "I longed for a mohair sweater; 'everyone' had one and many of my friends had several but Mom thought it was too frivolous, at least for me. I was raised to believe that I should be above caring about clothes, hairdos, girlish things. I see now that this attitude isolated me from most of the standard teenage activities. As an adult, I notice the pendulum has swung in the other direction. I may have trouble allowing myself to have pretty things, but I am an obsessive appreciator of others' finery.

"'It's always such a privilege to get one of your family,' the nuns would say. 'Your mother is a saint.' Singled out by the nuns as better than the other kids, I often felt isolated by this assigned virtue. It was a difficult identity for a young girl who yearned to belong to a peer group she was told did not exist for her."

She remembers packing her trunk the night she left for college and her mom looking in at the small stack of clothes and saying, "I never did buy you much, did I? I guess I never thought you needed them the way your sisters did." Julia says, "I was the caretaker child, always looking after my sisters, and I guess Mom just forgot I was a child at all."

That message evidently sank deeply into Julia's brain and defined a great deal of her self-image for years to come. She was the strong, brave, hardy, and independent girl who didn't need to have girly treats like other girls. Reactively, she prided herself on her bohemianism.

One particularly damaging form of isolation was her pre-dilection for cheap—dangerous—housing. Throughout Julia's twenties, she proudly discovered bargain apartments in border-line neighborhoods too frightening for her friends to visit.

So thoroughly had Julia learned the lessons her mother taught her that she had complete denial about any yearnings for luxury or niceties.

For Julia, all matters of money were matters of shame. She always felt she "should" be able to do better on less: less than what she had, less than what she needed, less than what many other people got or ever would have accepted.

"I know where it started," Julia claims. "I would do the family shopping for Mom and it was never done right. She always felt I could have been more frugal, more clever, more responsible. I've been trying to be that ever since."

## POVERTY AS SAINTHOOD

Cunning, baffling, and powerful, the money addiction some-times makes us paupers. Repelled by the materialism of the American Dream, we strive for lives of austerity, only to find we have crossed an invisible line and become addicted to self-deprivation.

Lack of money gets us high: we feel martyred, anxious, virtuous, self-righteous, and, yes, self-pitying. While smugly judging the "money-grubbing" all around us, we ourselves are ruled by money as well.

Obsessed with judgments of the shallowness around us, we fail to deepen and mature ourselves. In a sense, we remain chil-dren acted upon, not acting. Refusing to earn, to own, to hus-band and nurture our lives, we take spiritual pride in what amounts to an eternal adolescence, refusing to grow up and take responsibility for changing a system we may despise or accepting a world as it is and setting down roots. This would rob us of our position as outsiders, judges, and saints.

Seeking sainthood through her poverty, Helen, a psychologist, lives as though she were camping out, feeling she is somehow virtuous. She tells herself to "rise above" such petty feelings as comfort and material concerns. Helen compares herself to others, not those who spend more but those who spend less.

Yes, Helen knows her clothes are shabby—but they're not as shabby as her friend Ellen's. (Ellen is a welfare mother; Helen is a Poverty Addict. There's a difference, but Helen ignores it.)

True, there are times when she feels inappropriate, showing up at formal occasions in hand-me-down finery, wearing her sister's leftover dresses or her own college clothes 20 years out of date, but Helen tells herself such feelings are inappropriate. She clings to a sense of moral superiority that she wears like a sable coat.

The poverty addiction is also an addiction to hand wringing, to constant worry and complaint. Things are never going to be all right so why try to enjoy them now. If I can't have it all why have any of it? This attitude darkens our dreams and becomes an excuse for not living up to our potential for life, for the thrills of adventure and experience.

Caitlin is a Poverty Addict. She never has enough money; she never takes a job that pays her enough money. "Money is not a consideration," she tells herself when accepting a job. The truth is that money is often nearly all that she thinks about.

For a year, Caitlin worked at what she described to her friends as her "dream job." To their eyes, the dream looked like a nightmare. A talented commercial artist, Caitlin signed on to do graphics for a prestigious art magazine—a magazine so arty that its self-concept kept changing, and with each change in concept, a new set of graphics was required.

Caitlin tried to "be flexible." She tried to "be understanding" but often found herself doing the same job four times, four different ways while four different editors sought to find their artistic fulfillment at her expense. To her friends' increasing wonder and rage, Caitlin never seemed to reckon her own hourly costs. Overtime? No problem! Materials? She would cover them. Emotional wear and tear? They were all just part of the job. And they *were* all part of the job, *that* job.

As a Poverty Addict, it never occurred to Caitlin that she deserved better treatment. She counted herself lucky to have the job at all; she never stopped to reckon that the editors of the magazine were very, very lucky to have her in the job. All too often, avaricious and unprincipled employers are delighted to have a Poverty Addict in their employ.

## THE WAY OUT

For the way out of poverty addiction, it is very important that we begin to focus on what "delights" us and let ourselves have a little bit of that. All too often, a recovering Poverty Addict remains addicted to being "sensible." As a result, the new purchases are often as unattractive and as unappealing as the old.

Poverty Addicts need to unhook their sense of virtue from having no money and stop blocking their creativity with worry. What little self-worth Helen had, she fed with a sense of sainthood and competency achieved at her own expense. Undoing her financial anorexia, Helen had to allow herself the "luxury" of earning and spending money.

Chronically underpaid, Helen needed to learn to price her work appropriately. She needed to focus on the battered inner child she had long neglected.

Helen had to put thrift shop buying on the list of things she could no longer allow herself to do. She recognized that she had a dual addiction to the places. They fed both her miser's need for a bargain and her misplaced sense of moral righteousness as well.

"But I'll never be able to afford real clothes," she told her friends.

"We'll see," they answered.

What Helen saw, and quickly, was that she could afford "real" clothes and that as she began to allow herself to dress better she began, also, to treat herself better. For the first time in her life, Helen, herself, became a priority. Instead of overnurturing others, making sure they had what they needed while she went without, and undernourishing herself, she began to redress the balance; at first, by literally re-dressing herself.

For the recovering Poverty Addict, the act of spending can be very frightening. It is a learned behavior. Just as the Compulsive Spender (see Chapter Five) must learn to recognize and outlast the compulsion to overspend, the Poverty Addict must learn to recognize and outwit the compulsion to scrimp.

For Julia, as for many other recovering Poverty Addicts, it was necessary to set out minimums that she *must* spend in order to maintain a sense of health for herself. In each significant arena of her life, Julia set spending goals using the Prosperity Plan in Week Nine of the 90-Day Program to set up monthly clothing allowances, monthly entertainment allowances, monthly household allowances.

For the first time in her life, Julia was learning to spend appropriately, not "shrewdly." She bought groceries that left her not only fed but also nurtured—fresh raspberries, good bread.

She allowed herself a small bouquet of flowers each week, also good shampoo, "real" soap instead of bargain of the week. And, yes, she bought clothes. For the first time, Julia splurged on "extra" lingerie, a new dress she liked, not just needed.

For the money drunk recovering from a poverty addiction,

an unexpected shift in spiritual consciousness often occurs when
we begin self-nurturing. A universe (indeed a world) that had
long felt like a harsh and hostile place begins to be transformed
into a gentler and more loving habitat. Many recovering Poverty
Addicts have noted with some astonishment that as we begin to
give to ourselves, we begin, also, to receive unexpected gifts
from the universe.

This synchronicity often reinforces for the nonbeliever the
first, faint glimmerings of a faith. For the believer whose God
has been a vengeful one, well pleased by petty sacrifices, this
softening may result in an altered spiritual consciousness as well.
The way out is faith in a better future.

## ARE YOU A POVERTY ADDICT?

1. Do you think there is some virtue in being poor?

2. Do you forget to collect the monies owed to you?

3. Would a person with money wear anything you own?

4. Do you feel it is somehow more spiritual to be poor?

5. When you have more money, do you spend it on other
   people instead of yourself?

6. Do you underprice your skills or feel guilty about asking
   people to pay you for your work?

7. Do you deprive yourself of things you could really
   afford?

8. Do you pride yourself on living by your wits?

9. Do you lead a restricted life due to a lack of money?

10. Do you neglect the upkeep of your home since it's a dive
    anyway? Your car? Your clothes?

If you answered yes to any two of these questions, you may be a Poverty Addict.

If you answered yes to any three of these questions, you are probably a Poverty Addict.

If you answered yes to four or more of these questions, you can safely diagnose yourself as a Poverty Addict.

# CHAPTER
# 9

## THE CASH
## CO-DEPENDENT

Joan, a 33-year-old marketing manager, has been seeing her boyfriend, John, for almost two years. He is a Big Deal Chaser and has been without a paycheck almost the entire time while he worked on a big real estate deal. Joan supports him by lending him money for his rent, buying him clothes, and paying for dinner when they are out together. She also lets him use her car and has begun worrying about how to keep him from spending all her money.

Recently, Joan lost her job. Her savings, modest to begin with, are gone because she has taken care of John so long that she no longer has her own money for a rainy day. And he is unable to contribute.

She is going to work as a caterer while she looks for a career job (something John should consider doing), and she has been forced to move home with her parents in order to get back on her feet. Joan did not see her cash co-dependency in time to save her bank account. And, not surprisingly, John has a new love.

Just as alcoholism affects the nondrinkers in the family, the money addiction takes a toll on the family and friends of a money drunk by causing resentments and damaging the family's trust as they watch the money drunk get further and further into trouble. Battered by the roller coaster ride of violent mood swings brought about by the crisis of an active addiction, spouses, lovers, or family members may become so focused on the highs and lows of their loved one's finances that their own equilibrium suffers. When it does, they have become Cash Co-Dependents, and we are now dealing with two money drunks: the active money drunk whether Big Deal Chaser, Compulsive Spender, or even Poverty Addict, and the passive money drunk, the Cash Co-Dependent, the one who supplies the money to finance someone else's high rolling.

Like the wife of an alcoholic who drinks along with her husband, Cash Co-Dependents like Joan often buy into a money drunk's schemes. When the money drunk is out of work or spending extravagantly, the Cash Co-Dependent often digs deeper to cover the necessities the active money drunk ignores, thereby "enabling" him (or her) to stay drunk.

As much as we want to deny it, money has been as much an obsession for us as for our partner! All too often, we, too, have fallen prey to the "money is love" thinking we claim to despise. Why else would we find it so threatening to begin withholding what is rightfully *our* money?

The husband who "tolerates" a shopping habit allows his money drunk wife to continue her compulsive spending. The wife who takes a second job to "steady" the family finances may instead be cosigning further irresponsibility on her husband's part.

Chronically overworking to cover the spending of the active money drunk, the Cash Co-Dependents display all the symptoms of the Al-Anon side of the money addiction: excessive worry, attempts to control the other's spending, jeopardizing their own finances and well-being by giving money to the active addict, and attempting to repress plenty of anger that usually surfaces in passive-aggressive ways.

Yoked to the compulsive spending of our money drunk, our lives and our finances turn unmanageable. Left to our own devices, we can say no to overspending. Where we cannot say no is to our actively money drunk partner, and so, in effect, his or her financial irresponsibility, regardless of the cause, becomes our own.

Just like other types of money drunks, Cash Co-Dependents come in both sexes. Kevin, struggling to get on his feet as an artist, complicated the process for himself by marrying a Compulsive Spender. Natalie loved Kevin and wanted him to pursue his art but she needed him to make a good living to support her spending sprees. Hooked by small-stakes gambling, Natalie began by playing bingo and then moved on. She joined sports pools, betting at the office. She pleaded to take a few junkets to the track. Kevin, neither money drunk nor a gambler himself, could take or leave such expeditions. To his wife, they were a way to stop time in its tracks. Gambling made her feel young, wild, daring. She needed that high.

As it always had, spending altered her mood. Gambling, her preferred form of spending, gave her a jolt of adrenaline. It made her feel truly alive. Yes, Natalie needed to gamble, and Kevin, her Cash Co-Dependent, needed to find the money to help her do it, to alleviate his fears of being left alone, and feeling somehow unworthy.

With a money addiction to feed, Kevin began to lie to Natalie about how much money he had, feeling that he had to baby-sit her spending. Soon, he could no longer afford the vagaries of a fledgling artist's life and setting aside his dream, and he turned his creativity to a corporate job where his paycheck was secure—but ultimately not large enough to secure him Natalie.

As Natalie's spending accelerated, she badgered him to ask for raises, to work free-lance on the side. "My God," he said to her one night, "you're like a junkie without morals. This habit of yours is killing us and I'm helping you do it."

With that moment of clarity, Kevin began to look for answers to why he could not say no to Natalie. If he could not save her or the marriage, he could at least begin to save himself. He went for help. Not all of us have such courage.

## ACCEPTING RESPONSIBILITY

For many a Cash Co-Dependent, the clarity to seek help is hard to find. There is quite a payoff in being the long-suffering loyal supporter of a beleaguered "bad luck" spouse. (We can blame all our misfortunes on him or her, and not have to take responsibility ourselves.) Then, too, there is the fact that the money addiction itself keeps us off center.

All money drunks have periods of seeming stability during which the Cash Co-Dependent is lulled into re-entering denial. "This time will be different," we say, mistaking the calm between storms for a real change in climate. We believe what we want to believe.

Of course we do. . . .

For the Cash Co-Dependent, her mate's money-related mood swings constitute a brutal treadmill. If he's a Big Deal Chaser, then, cash in hand, he's a great guy. Broke, he's miserable to live with. If he's a Poverty Addict, his refusal to enjoy life can leave the marriage dull and listless. If he's a Maintenance Money Drunk, she will get tired of hearing the same old woes.

Like alcoholics deprived of liquor, money drunks down on their luck arc hard people to handle. Blame and self-pity enter the air and hover like a chill cloud. Money drunks like to blame others for their troubles and lament their bad luck.

"I don't need you or your money," "you or your bullying," "you or your outside activities," the money drunk snaps when his or her actions are questioned. Such protestations do little to reassure.

As Cash Co-Dependents, we may need to keep a very close eye on the little ways we learn to manipulate those around us. All too often we find that we use treats as tiny bribes. After a fight, we may buy a little something to soothe troubled waters. We may trick them into coming outdoors, or taking a new class for their own good. Actions like these are like offering an alcoholic a beer to nurse a hangover; they start the whole cycle over again.

Instead of the self-worth we get by taking care of ourselves appropriately, we get the quick fix of self-worth from helping others to feel dependent on us.

"Is he after my money?" the Cash Co-Dependent starts to wonder, counting back over the loans, the joint ventures to cheer him or her up and onward.

Leigh is 60 years old and lives on Social Security and $400 a month from her divorce settlement after 28 years of marriage. Recently an inheritance from her mother's death gave her a sum of $28,000 in cash. It was enough to buy a car and make a down payment on a modest place to live. Soon, the trust would begin to pay her $1,000 a month and it looked as though Leigh, a woman who had worked hard all her life, was finally going to have a place of her own.

Then Leigh's son William called from Texas. William is 32 years old, has never had a dime in savings, and continues to treat his parents like a loan organization. He was on the skids again and needed just enough money to pay his back rent and phone bills. Leigh knows William's fatal flaw is his money madness but she gave him the money, even though her other sons warned her not to, and after three months, Leigh had "loaned" William $10,500, all the money she had left.

Leigh never got her own place to live. She even had to get a loan on her car in order to rent an apartment. William was, as his brothers predicted, unable to keep his house, even with his mother's money. (Remember that for a money drunk there is never enough money.)

Everyone is back to where they started. William is still broke, except that he owes his mother more money he can't pay. And Leigh never got her house.

For cash Co-Dependents like Leigh and Joan, the beginning of solvency must be preceded by a final declaration of defiance—"I will not lend that SOB one more cent"—followed by the acceptance of responsibility for their own actions. They must cease to blame the active money drunk for "taking their money," and look at why they gave it to them in the first place.

In other words, the Cash Co-Dependent, like the Al-Anon spouse of a practicing alcoholic, must accept his or her own role in the exchange and break the cycle of addictive behavior, instead asking for the help needed to start doing the things that matter, which is taking care of him or herself first, and learning to say no to others' demands.

## THE WAY OUT

For the Cash Co-Dependent, recovery may at first look, and will certainly feel, *selfish*. Long accustomed to placing others' financial needs before our own, we find it difficult to think about spending money on ourselves when there are others who need it more. Using the Prosperity Plan from Week Nine of the 90-Day Program helps us to monitor our own needs first and to begin to set limits for ourselves. The Time Grid from Week Ten begins to help us set boundaries for self-nurturance, and the Money Buddy from Week Seven gives us someone we can talk to who knows our exact situation and can nudge us when we start wanting to take care of someone else.

For many Cash Co-Dependents, the help of a co-dependency group is invaluable. While money addiction differs from alcoholism in its substance of choice for the abuser, it creates remarkably similar patterns of behavior in the significant other.

Like Al-Anon spouses, Cash Co-Dependents are often plagued by feelings of martyrdom and an overdeveloped sense of duty. Without really admitting it to ourselves, we tend to view our money drunk partners as children whom we must control "for their own good."

A truth that is often reluctantly faced is that we Cash Co-Dependents can be quite addicted to feeling superior. After all, *we* can handle *our* money. But can we?

A close look at our own finances often reveals that we have co-signed foolish schemes rather than risk losing our lovers. We have used money to manipulate our relationships. We have hidden it, lied about it, gone "terminally vague" rather than admit we open our own finances to the mismanagement of our spouses. We may have ruined our own credit ratings, used our own savings, denied our own dreams in order to finance the dreams and schemes of our loved ones, and in the process become bitter, cynical people.

For the Cash Co-Dependent, the way out may entail some rigorous recordkeeping. Exactly where is our money going? Many of us find that we spend our money to compensate for our broke partners. When they are tapped out, we routinely pick up the slack, rather than allow them the discomfort of feeling their real financial status. This overspending to help our partners is enabling them to keep denying their financial situation. It hurts them and it hurts us.

"How we treat ourselves tells other people how to treat us," the old saying goes. In recovery, Cash Co-Dependents must first face the truth of this and then treat themselves better. We start finding a self to like. We start learning to say No. We learn that treating ourselves like a precious object will make us strong.

## ARE YOU A CASH CO-DEPENDENT?

1. Do you co-sign foolish plans even when you feel you know better?

2. Do you feel money robs your partner of his or her normal moral values?

3. Have you worried about how to protect your own assets in your relationship?

4. Do you lie to your partner and tell him or her you have less money than you do?

5. Are you deliberately vague about where your money goes so that your partner won't lay claim to spending it?

6. Are you afraid that your partner or members of your family see you chiefly as a bank or a loan organization?

7. Are you afraid to say no to your partner about money?

8. Do you consider "money madness" your partner's fatal flaw?

9. Do you feel you have to baby-sit his or her spending?

10. Do you often complain to friends or family about your partner's money habits?

If you answered yes to any two of these questions, you may be a Cash Co-Dependent.

If you answered yes to any three questions, you are probably a Cash Co-Dependent.

If you answered yes to four or more of these questions, you can safely diagnose yourself as a Cash Co-Dependent.

# THREE

*The Solution*

# THE 90-DAY
# PROGRAM

In our teaching, we prefer working with a 90-day time frame, which is the traditional time frame used by support groups for changing behavior. (AA groups often recommend a newcomer go to 90 meetings in 90 days.) If you can do something steadily for three months, whether it be exercising, studying a language, learning an instrument, or counting your money, you are well on your way to beginning a new pattern of behaving and, thus, thinking. Too often people try to alter thinking while chaotic behavior continues to confuse them. We have found that if you change the behavior, the attitudes you hold about that behavior will become apparent, and you can then work with them at depth.

For years, Marie resisted balancing her checkbook or even recording her checks. When we insisted she needed to do this, Marie blurted out, "But I like the excitement of never quite knowing and besides my math is bad." A conservative woman, Marie was astonished by her own attitude. It reminded her all too clearly of her money drunk, devil-may-care father.

Fred, another student, resisted writing down his expenditures. "Come on," we urged him, "You'll find out you have more money than you think you do, you've just been misappropriating it." Reluctantly, Fred began counting only to complain, "I liked it better when I thought I was really broke. Now my only excuse for no food in my refrigerator is low self-care."

The following program arrests money-drunk behavior, examines its extent, and initiates a rapid solution. For convenience we have divided the program into 12 weeks (84 days), with a final 6 days being devoted to examining and celebrating your progress and to developing a personal vision for your future. Some of the exercises in the beginning of the program will continue for the entire 90 days (and beyond), and some will be done just once or perhaps occasionally throughout the three months. Please do not worry about or question the activities. Just do them; they will work.

The program is divided into three sections:

- Weeks One to Four: Awareness.
  The tools presented in this section—Counting and Time Out, Abstinence, Inventory, and the Bottom Line—are designed to make you aware of your habits in very specific detail and to help you learn where your money currently comes from and where it goes. We are not judging anything in these weeks, merely learning about our situations with money much the way a scientist would examine a new problem. To recover fiscally, we have to know what elements we are dealing with. The tools in this section may cause us both relief and distress because they expose our denial. (After these weeks, the worst will be over and you will have survived!)

- Weeks Five to Eight: Acceptance.
  This section's tools—the Money Map, the Resource List, the Money Buddy, and the Freedom Accounts—are dedi-

cated to accepting the situations we have discovered in our investigations and beginning to take responsibility for our continued solvency. What is our financial reality? How much do we make? Where do we spend it? What are our shortfalls? What inner resources do we possess to move us forward? Whom can we count on for support and guidance? All of these questions will be answered in this section.

- Weeks Nine to Twelve: Action.

These weeks present our plan for the future. By this time we shall have come out of darkness and ended the ambiguity in our dealings with money. With a newfound confidence in our ability to act wisely on our own behalf, we will be breathing easier. Soon we will begin to plan, dust off our dreams, and formulate long-term goals. These tools—the Prosperity Plan, the Time Grid, the Relapse Checklist, and Spirituality—help us to discover what we really want in our lives and how to get it, one day at a time. This section begins to turn wishes into goals and, most important, focuses on living *now,* being happy *now,* and gaining a sense of peace and abundance in our lives from this day forward.

Finally, the chapter we call Vision will help you to appreciate who you are and to give you a solid foundation for accepting the inevitable changes that life and solvency bring.

## GETTING FROM AWARENESS TO ACTION

As money drunks on the way out of financial darkness, we learn the use of some simple tools that will change the way we think (and act) about money and will help us no matter how poor we are, how unmanageable our money is, or how little we learned from our parents.

In the following exercises we separate the skeptics from those money drunks who are ready for recovery. For it is here that you have to really dig in and begin the work of getting solvent. A description of a hammer will never be as satisfying as striking the blow that sends a nail solidly into wood. A description of the tools in the 90-Day Program will never be as satisfying, or persuasive, as using them yourself. You have come this far; do not turn back now.

Experience has taught us that recovery hinges not only on changed attitudes *but changed actions as well.* It is our hope that the pages of this book have inspired you with a sense of commitment and excitement about using the tools we describe.

It is an old joke that self-realization is always bad news. And no doubt some of these next weeks, particularly the first few, may feel like bad news. Do not be discouraged. All we are doing is looking at the situation as it stands until we can see it clearly. You do not need to change anything just yet.

As a money drunk, you are faced with a complicated problem that has a simple solution. Right now, it does not matter *why* your relationship to money is so destructive. If you are in a burning house, you do not ask how the fire started before you run for help. Save the psychological questions for later. For now, get yourself out of the fire.

Above all, know that there is a way out and that there are many, many people who have traveled this path. There *is* something you can do. We will tell you in very concrete terms the step-by-step methods that we and many others have used to get money sober. You may wish to read straight through the program and then begin at the beginning. Or start right away, it's up to you.

In each of the sections we'll explain (and establish) a list of activities and tools. But for now we want to introduce the most important recovery tool: the "No-Fault Rule." Put simply, the No-Fault Rule means that while we now accept responsibility for our financial situation, we no longer accept shame for it.

Yes, we have money problems.

No, *we* are not our money problems.

No matter how painful, shameful, or troubled our pasts have been, our pasts are our *pasts*. What we are dealing with now is the present, a new day that will lead to a solvent future. The key to truly changing our behaviors around money is using the tools provided.

COUNTING AND
TIME OUT:
THE
RECOVERY
OF CLARITY

## COUNTING

Counting is the most basic tool for gaining clarity. When we spend, we count the amount. And when we make money we count that too. Money in—money out.

Counting. The exercise is just that. We're just looking, thank you. No need to fix anything, no need to be cross, no need to beat ourselves up about it. That's not the plan. We just want to see where it goes. Easy. Simple. Old-fashioned.

As simple as it appears, this tool yields us a remarkable degree of information and control.

Counting shows us how much—or how little—we take care of ourselves. For many of us, life's proportions are off; we over-work and underplay. We overplay and underwork. We binge on new fashion but starve ourselves intellectually. Or we are gluttons for books but won't give ourselves a nice shirt.

We throw away money on expensive dinners but never use the cash to buy a good mattress/a decent reading chair/some new sheets. These discoveries about our misdirected spending can frighten us at first. We are often shocked by how poorly we have been treating ourselves.

What we will be aiming for, eventually, is a healthy balance—and not just in our checkbook. By counting our expenditures, seeing where we overspend and where we cruelly skimp (money drunks often don't even have a clothing allowance), we begin to sense the balance in our lives, the balance in our relationships, the balance in our work, the balance in our creative endeavors, the balance of our days.

Writing down an "impulse" buy may soon abort the unnecessary ones. "Wait a minute. Do I really need this?" we may catch ourselves thinking. But for now just start doing it.

Solvency is a process. No judging allowed. We are going to get better. But first, we must count what we spend. Remember, this is an exercise, not an inquisition.

So, get a notepad, and let's get started. No, we don't need to start at the first of the month. Today is perfect. This is not high finance, not economics—just learning to count. (Debtors Anonymous calls this process of writing down all your expenditures "recording"). So don't be scared (although you may be). It's easy. It's fun. (At least it *will* be.) And it's a very old trick.

The notepad should be small, about the size of a wallet, pocket-size. Some people even keep their money inside it, inside their pocket or purse, so they will always have the notepad handy when they pay for anything. Most cash registers have pens nearby, so if you forget yours, just say: "Can I borrow a pen?" Write down your purchase and give the clerk back the pen.

Mark remembers: "The first month I started counting I couldn't believe that I had lived 15 years as an adult and never knew how much it cost me to live each month or where my money went. Then, one day while I was standing at the checkout counter and got my book out to write down the amount of my purchase, an old guy standing near me said, 'You know, when I was young all the old-timers used to do that.'"

Mark laughs. "I was amazed. It wasn't such a new idea after all. I felt more secure somehow that it was an age-old technique. It felt somehow more viable."

The first month Julia was counting she noticed she spent $184 on books. "Good," you might think, "a real intellectual." Julia saw something else. "I hide in books," she discovered. "I was saying I had no money to go to the theater, but the truth was I had plenty of money. All I had to do was go *see* a play instead of buying one to read."

*Counting* all of our expenditures will teach us a lot about ourselves.

Now, at the end of the month, you will know exactly how much you spent for groceries (even what day you spent it), how much you spent in diners, how much money you lent your brother, gave your sister, spent on flowers, cabs, travel, tips, clothes . . . everything.

And it's not so hard. People have been doing it for a long time. It works like this: We write down everything we spend, and what we spend it for. We also write down everything we make. Simple. Money in, money out. We list the amount of our income (whether it be paycheck or daily tips, or the occasional free-lance check, or an IRS refund, anything we make) and the day it came in. We will use this to help us time our expenditures and keep track of our checkbooks. Financial clarity can change our lives.

## TIME OUT

For most recovering money drunks it is necessary to declare a "Time Out." Typically, a Time Out lasts from one to several months and is used to stabilize our finances.

During our Time Out, we call the creditors we owe and assure them of our intent to pay at some future time. In this way, we keep the sharks from eating us alive.

During a time out, we:

1. Refrain from debting (see Abstinence from Week Two).

2. Avoid big new expenses.

3. Inform creditors who are hounding us of our intent to pay. (Stop hiding.)

The Time Out is a recovery technique intended to buy us time to think and plan. Battered by our active money addictions, we need time to normalize our adrenaline-altered perceptions. Remember, we are money *drunks*. Ours has been a long and damaging bender.

Just as a drunk is not truly sober while in the throes of a massive hangover, we money drunks are not truly sober in the early stages of our recovery. It takes time for our vision to adjust to reality. Hence, we urge a Time Out rather than an immediate binge of frantic actions.

Just as the alcoholic must quit drinking to see his drinking problems clearly, we money drunks must stop robbing Peter to pay Paul before financial clarity can be ours. (This is often a gradual realization of the truth.)

A compulsive behavior like a money addiction (or drinking) reaches its tentacles into all areas of our life. Our businesses. Our friendships. Our families. Our children. As we abstain from our compulsive behavior, we gain health in all the areas that it affected.

## JANE'S TIME OUT

When Jane entered recovery, she was mad as hell about it. She didn't want to look at her finances but she could no longer tolerate the pain they were causing her, either. When it was suggested she try a Time Out to take inventory for herself, Jane recoiled in utter terror.

"I can't take time out. If I do, it will ruin my credit rating."

For the past six months, Jane had already been taking time out, just not officially. Unable to meet even the barest minimum on her cards, she had resigned herself to collection calls from the credit card companies and kept her answering machine on even when she was home.

Instead of making her feel better, this avoidance actually made her feel worse. She hated to play her message tape back. She hated it so much that she didn't do it. Soon her friends began to complain that they left messages but got no return calls from her.

"My machine's been on the blink," Jane fibbed. This fibbing made her feel nearly as bad as the calls from creditors did.

Jane felt trapped. Emotionally, she felt unable to deal with the pressures her acting-out with money had caused for her. If she did pick up the phone and talk to a creditor, she inevitably promised to send them whatever they asked, only to know she could not keep the promise and had once again lied.

Jane's friends in money recovery advised her: "Tell them you will pay them, just not now. Take the initiative, call your creditors, and tell them you are in a financial recovery and will get back to them in 90 days with your plan for repayment."

To Jane's ear, such advice sounded haywire. She only tried it because she felt she had no choice. Her own "plan" was certainly not working. The deeper she buried her head in the sand, the more suffocated she felt. And so, she did as her new friends advised her.

To Jane's surprise, she was met with open ears, if not open arms. Her creditors applauded her honesty and her efforts at stabilization. While not precisely enthusiastic, they were no longer adversarial. Jane's display of honest intent to pay went a long way toward calming the waters.

## ACTIVITIES

**1.** Get a small notebook.

**2.** Write down any—and all—daily expenditures, and any and all monies in. Everything you spend should be written down and counted. How much you spent, what day it was, and what the item was. Continue this exercise for the entire 90 days. Try not to miss a day. You will count like this every day for 90 days.

**EXAMPLE:**                                    **Income**

| Jan 3 | $  .35 newspaper | $395.00—job |
|-------|------------------|-------------|
|       | $ 4.00 breakfast |             |
|       | $ 1.50 tip       |             |
|       | $ 2.00 subway    |             |
|       | $20.00 groceries |             |

## CAUTIONS:

**A.** Don't judge yourself or your spending. We are just looking.

**B.** Don't be surprised if this is hard to do at first. (If you have trouble, just start with the next purchase.)

**3.** Take a Time Out. Stop promising things you cannot do. (Explain to those who ask that you will pay them when you are sure of your situation. This will be within 90 Days.)

**4.** Answer all your mail, with a phone call at least. (You will make plans for repayment in Week Eight.)

# ABSTINENCE:
# THE
# RECOVERY
# OF DIGNITY

Abstinence is the primary tool for getting out of debt. One day at a time we do not incur any new debt or use credit. We stop debting. While this may seem more a nonaction than an action, it is the one and only action to stop the debt spiral. On this simple cornerstone, new lives and new self-respect are built.

In our experience, "not debting" is such a simple tool that people often fail to credit themselves with using it. They stop debting and instantly focus on debt repayment. They miss the fact that they have halted a progressive disaster and are now involved with damage control. They focus on the fact that the disaster happened instead of on the fact that it has now *stopped* happening and can be repaired.

An analogy will help us to explain. Let us say that while we are debting our life is a leaking boat and that boat is sinking. When we stop debting and begin to practice abstinence, our boat stops leaking. Now we focus on bailing out.

Just as the alcoholic in early recovery may still not understand that abstinence from alcohol means *total* abstinence—no beer at the ball game, no wine with dinner, no shot of whiskey for a cold—we money drunks may find financial abstinence equally incomprehensible.

No more debt means, simply, no more debt. (A debt is any unsecured loan for which we offer no collateral. For our purposes, therefore, loans for cars or houses are okay.) It's time for pay as you go, cash and carry. Time for, "Sorry, I can't do that right now." Time for, "What bills *must* I cover? What can wait?" And then waiting.

Abstinence means no more borrowing from friends, bosses, credit cards. No more spending the rent money while telling yourself you will catch up later. No more spending ahead on the deal that's sure to close.

For the money drunk, the first debt starts the debting spiral. One day at a time, we must abstain from debting to attain our solvency.

For alcoholics accustomed to fighting to control their drinking, the news that it is the first drink that gets them drunk is often—incredibly—exactly that: *news.*

"I thought it was the seventh or eighth drink," a newly sober AA may say, amazed. We money drunks feel the same way. Abstinence is not something we easily understand.

No debting? *No Debting.* That means no contracting for services we can't afford now. That means no checks floating on expected funds. No "running accounts" with our doctors, our grocers, our department stores.

"Pay now or don't acquire it" is one way to put it. Or, more colloquially: If you ain't got it—don't get it.

As we begin to practice the principle of not debting, we may move into a new area of recovery: withdrawal. For many of us, the withdrawal from our active money addiction may be characterized by the feeling we're going crazy. In point of fact, we're going sane—and that feels "crazy" to us.

Because of the intensity of the feelings brought on by this tool, we include in this chapter some empathy on withdrawal and a few activities specifically to help you nurture yourself during this "period of adjustment." One of the main emotions to emerge at this time is anger. Our advice is: use it.

## WITHDRAWAL: THE USE OF ANGER

You slam the car door. Hard. You bark at your lover for no apparent reason. You stomp out of the house because "someone" put the ice cube trays back empty.

What's going on?

Anger. Anger is what's going on. A lot of anger. Anger and more anger and even more anger than that.

Why?

Withdrawal. You are withdrawing from a lifestyle/a death style/a world view/an addiction/an obsession/a compulsion/a long, lurid drunk.

For years, you have used money (or the lack of it) to block your feelings, and now those blocked feelings are tumbling out. And out. And out. . . .

"I'm angry at being taken for granted . . . I'm angry about being overused and underpaid." Or, perhaps, "I am angry at being overpaid and underused."

For many of us, debt masked our rage. Worried about being evicted, who had time to worry about our trampled convictions? Worried about the phone bill, who focused on the friend who never called?

The money drunk struck sober is suddenly hungry for balance, and not just in the checkbook. We want reciprocity. Respect. A return of appreciation for services rendered.

Please and thank you. Courtesy. Tit for tat. We are hungry to be acknowledged. No longer the butt of "friendly jokes," no longer our very own, portable punch line, we find self-respect no laughing matter. Suddenly, sharply, we *care* how we are treated. We care so much, we are angry.

The anger feels like fire in the gut. Hiroshima behind the eyes. It's scary, this anger. It's not "nice." We've been nice too long. Unable to pay our own way we have relied on charm to bribe us through life. We had to "be nice." We had to "make nice." We had to "act nice."

We knew someday, someday soon, we would need a favor. And so, we said, "It's okay," when it really wasn't. We said, "Don't worry about it," when *we* worried. We said, "It's no problem," when it was one. The problem (our inability to handle our finances) was big, and it was ours.

Worried about whether we'd get credit at all, we bought a car we didn't like. And if it didn't run properly, we just "made do" rather than complain.

As practicing money drunks, we didn't even feel safe at home—dunning notices in the mail, unwelcome and unpleasant phone calls that harassed us and disturbed our self-worth: these were the rule, not the exception.

Struck sober, we now take exception to all of it. Every bit of it makes us mad. In truth it always did, but we just didn't acknowledge it.

We didn't acknowledge a lot of things. When the ceiling leaked, our self-esteem leaked with it. Behind on the rent, afraid to ask for services, we made do because we were afraid that if we said anything, eviction was sure to follow.

Paid up, we suddenly find we are fed up as well. We suddenly see the peeling plaster, the windows not up to code, the paint job not up to snuff. When we get a good look at what we've scttled for, it is very unsettling. Withdrawal is a difficult passage no matter what the addiction.

Our anger feels volcanic. It feels nuclear. It feels explosive. Of course it does: our anger is fuel.

Once we realize this, we can use it. And we do.

We're up at dawn scrubbing the floor. At midnight, we're still sorting the bookshelves, tossing out papers. All the energy we've invested in all those years of crisis management has suddenly boomeranged back into our own domain. (Unless recognized for what it is, this new energy can feel like yet another crisis.) And it almost is a crisis, just to manage it.

This is withdrawal.

We withdraw the energy we have spent on making nice and making do and we begin to invest it in ourselves. We mend the torn sheets, we glue the rickety chairs, hammer the doorjamb back straight. We get busy, busy, *busy*. On our own behalf.

Accustomed to the tornado of financial disaster, we hang on for dear life now as we ride out the swirling winds of change that are recovery. Even when our externals—house, job, family life—remain the "same," they may feel very different. They feel different because *we* are what's changing. And when *we* change, everything else does too.

"No," we say, asked for a favor that's out of line.

No? This may be a new one coming from us.

"I really don't want to!" we shout when pressed too far. Our friends recoil. Who is this angry stranger?

We wonder that ourselves.

"I won't be henpecked!" shouts the badgered husband, meek for years because his money mismanagement had mangled his sense of manhood.

"I deserve a dinner out! And even dancing!" bursts out the long-time martyred Cash Co-Dependent woman, who is newly solvent and placing her own needs first for once. She's spent her time and money and energy on her loved ones for so many years that they have never realized it was *her* time and *her* money and *her* energy that *they* were spending. For the first time she sees herself as deserving a treat or two. How dare she?

"I've had all I can take of your sloppiness!" we shout at children we've served like maids, waiting on them hand and foot instead of raising them to be responsible.

"Clean your own room! Pitch in around here! I am not Cinderella!"

Our spouses may be stunned. Our children may resent us. Our friends may not find us so friendly any longer. Can we really get through all this? Is this really healthy? What the hell is happening?

It's a time of transition, we tell ourselves. We're changing rapidly. Will they?

Small victories are big deals to us. We have an ATM card again. We're proud and a little bit nervous. We still may try to monkey with the system and get cash out we don't truly have. The checkbook is balanced—and so are we, but it's a balancing act that takes a lot of attention. Every day without debting feels like a big deal. We are digging out, a little at a time at first, just by not digging ourselves any deeper into debt.

Small slights are a big deal to us, too. Newly self-respecting, we're touchy. All those years of trampled self-worth have left us a little bruised.

"No. I won't tell you it's okay you threw my shirt on the floor. It *is* a big deal to me," we storm.

Forced to the wall by our sudden changes, our intimates may feel cornered—and may retaliate. The spoiled child may sulk or lash out. Like a heat-seeking missile, the self-righteous spouse anxiously may find new faults in us to criticize.

The lover who once seemed perfect may not look that way

any longer. We see she drags her feet about pulling her own weight. Of course she does. We trained her to believe we would tolerate anything.

"You're too dependent!" we hear ourselves yelling at people whose very dependency we encouraged because we loved its safety when our own self-worth was low.

With our self-esteem rising, our expectations percolate upward too. Now we demand of ourselves and others a level of self-sufficiency that was daunting before.

"Fold your own laundry!" we snap at the spouse lounging while we toil.

"I could use some help!" we snap at the ravenous family members slinking like wolves through the kitchen when the table still needs setting. "Set the table! Pour the milk! Pitch in around here!"

We have a new motto. "Lead, follow, or get out of the way!" We're ready to roll now and sometimes we steamroll others. Out with the old life! In with the new! Adrenaline surges where fear used to jump-start our days.

Angered by our lost years, we hate to lose a single minute now. This is when "Easy Does It" feels like an insult instead of a prescription for health.

Sudden fits of weeping; bursts of euphoria; sleep that the dead would envy, it's so deep; more withdrawal.

"Easy does it?" we shout. "Easy for you to say!"

Working to catch up, we forget to play. Burning with angers old and new, we risk burning out unless we feed ourselves as well as the flames of change.

"Nurture yourself. Slow down. Spoil yourself a little," friends who are further into fiscal recovery tell us. Against our better judgment, we try it a little—and we feel a little better.

In recovery, anger is a road map that we learn how to read. "I hate my house." What, specifically, do you hate? Change that.

"I hate my life." What, specifically, would improve it?

You can't change generalities, but you can deal with specifics one on one. In withdrawal, use your rage to arm-wrestle doable things.

Do: clear out the closets; throw out the dead files; clean the kitchen; toss out old shabby clothing; take a class in what interests you. Exercise your body and your options.

Remember, anger is fuel. Use it.

Where is yours taking you? Steer the car. Head the way you'd like to, even though the road may be bumpy. Fender-benders with friends and family may be frequent, but progress is real. Look at that map of yours.

True North is where you're heading. You're traveling toward home—to the life you want, you choose, and you aim for.

---

**ACTIVITIES FOR AWARENESS**

**1.** Do not debt. One day at a time, for the whole 90 days. Keep track of any times you do debt, to see when and why you did it. How were you feeling? What was going on in your life that day? Can you see a pattern?

**2.** Watch for money stories in the paper and on television. Clip them out. Start a file. (It helps break the feeling we are alone and teaches us how pervasive the money addiction is.) Do this for one week.

**3.** Buy the supermarket tabloids. (They are great for money stories.) List five stories about the financial powerlessness of others. (This shows us we're not the worst.) Do this for one week.

**4.** List five people whose uncontrolled spending toppled them. (Any news show or paper should provide great stories.) Do this at least once.

**5.** Inventory your own types of debting behaviors. Do you:
Borrow ahead on paychecks?
Borrow from friends?
Live on credit cards?
Write checks on expected funds?
Charge your basic services like rent or utility bills?
Having trouble charging for your work? (This is a debt to yourself.)
Keep this list. We will use it later. Do this once. Add anything that comes up later.

**6.** Exercise. Take 20-minute walks every day for the whole 90 days if possible.

**7.** Take hot baths when you are feeling anxious.

**8.** Get extra sleep.

**9.** Go over your counting. How did you do? Pretty accurate? Small mistakes are okay for now, but they may aggravate you later after you find comfort in knowing where your money went. Do this weekly throughout the 90 days.

Inventory and
Keeping
a Journal:
# THE
# RECOVERY OF
# AUTHENTICITY

## INVENTORY

In order to become authentic (trustworthy), it is important that we conduct a "fearless and searching" inventory of our actions with money, both good and bad.

"It is impossible to get better and look good at the same time," the saying goes. Yet looking good is an obsession for many of us. The effort to keep up appearances masks how we *really* are and what we really feel. Ultimately, it keeps us stuck.

We money drunks can be charmers—cons—and we con ourselves the most. We fib a little and smile a lot. We won't face the money, the bills, the creditors. We won't face the necessary pain that allows us to struggle through to a balanced reality.

When friends say, "You're not sixteen anymore," we discount them for being on their high horse. This is our grandiosity, another potent defense. How dare they question *us*?

When a family member asks, "How are you doing?" we say, *"Fine."* We tell ourselves we'd better be fine since no one wants to hear about our phone bills, our rent payments, our lapsed car insurance.

"It's not good to be too depressed," we think. "Life is supposed to be fun." The happy face is a potent form of denial, the "It's okay" lie we tell ourselves when it's not.

As practicing money drunks, envy is our constant companion. We just know that everybody else is having more fun than we are. They really *are* happy and, we tell ourselves, "I'd better act as if I'm happy if I want to be accepted." No one likes a killjoy, let alone someone who's broke, too. But too often our happy face keeps us from facing (and thus overcoming) our pain.

Putting on our happy face, we money drunks tell ourselves it is the only one that can be used in public. It is also the only one we can bear to wear in private. Our motto is "Grin and bear it," not "Grin and *bare* it." The first requirement of recovery is self-disclosure. And these lessons can be difficult.

As we have been teaching and printing out these materials in various forms for our students, we have used a local print shop for copying, faxes, binding materials, computer paper, and pens. For a long time, we just figured it as a business expense and ran up a tab. Then we began to let the tab get bigger and bigger until suddenly it was a thousand dollars. That was not fair to our program of abstinence, to our printer, or even to ourselves, because it kept us from watching the exact charges as they were compiled. Our ongoing inventory showed us this problem. We pay cash at the printer now.

Another thing the inventory can help us see is when we are using blame instead of action. When we first started teaching in the larger groups, often over 100 people, it was confusing and embarrassing to ask for money. When some people did not pay us, we blamed them. "They're not living up to their part of the bargain." What we realized was that as teachers we had a responsibility to ourselves to collect the money or ask the students to make other arrangements. It was our job to ensure that they followed through. We have now made payment books in which everything is in writing from the beginning. Everyone knows what is expected from them and what the consequences are for not meeting these expectations.

Ask yourself how often you have taken the "easier, softer way" around money and not gotten a deal in writing. The old rule among lawyers is, "If a man is willing to say it, he ought to be willing to put it on paper and sign his name beside it." To get deals in writing was just one more thing we learned from our inventory.

The following inventory will help you to know yourself better and to pinpoint trouble areas in which you need work. It is intended to shatter denial and establish reality, but remember it is also a tool to discover and enhance your strengths. Don't forget the positive side of your situation and your character.

This inventory is meant to illuminate the areas in which we are most competent and those in which we are weakest. This will allow us to focus on our strengths and begin to shore up our weaknesses.

## KEEPING A JOURNAL

Another problem that confuses many of us money drunks is the expression of emotions. Often the roller coaster of our money addiction has contributed to our emotional binges causing us to rage uncontrollably or to drown in depression and self-pity. And more times than not we did not know *what* we were really feeling or what set us off.

We have found that keeping a daily journal of our thoughts, emotions, and activities leads us into further clarity about what we really feel and think. As you conduct the inventory this week start writing down your private thoughts and feelings and keep them in your notebook. Keep a journal for the remainder of the 90 days, trying to stay with it daily. Give it 20 minutes (or at least two pages) a day minimum. It will make a very informative and rewarding record of your way out.

(Hint: if you are angry and don't know why, write about it. If you are feeling like quitting, write about it; if you are depressed and can't seem to pull out of it, write about it; if you can't sleep at night, get up and write; if you can't keep track of what you have to do, make a list; if you are debting and can't stop, write about it; if you are not counting your money, write about it; and if you can't seem to make yourself ask for guidance, write about that. A daily journal is one of the most powerful tools in the world for building wisdom and it is an ancient custom.)

## STRENGTHS AND WEAKNESSES INVENTORY

Start a notebook for the following work so that you might add things later and still have the following exercises for reference.

1. List five times you have felt powerless in your spending. This helps break denial.

2. List five efforts you have made to control your spending. This also helps overcome denial.

3. What was your very first job? Where was it? How much did you make? Reminisce a little. Just for fun.

4. List every job you've had, in chronological order. How much did you make at each one? What did you like? Why did you leave? What did you dislike? This is to help us realize that we really have tried to work for a living.

5. List all the incidents of financial instability you can recall. Another denial breaker.

6. List all measures you have taken to recover on your own (e.g., therapy, financial consultants).

7. Ask yourself, "In what ways have my attitudes and actions around money hurt me? Hurt my family?"

8. Has money ever been part of a relapse of another addiction? This is an early warning system.

9. How would you feel right now, if all your money problems were gone? Sit quietly and imagine it. All the bills paid, savings in the bank, regular income. Try to feel the same feelings as if it were true. (This is a preview of what is in store.)

10. How has your counting been going? Are you able to be consistent? Have you been unwilling to write your expenditures down? If so, just relax and right now take a pen and see if you can reconstruct today's spending. It won't take a minute.

11. Go through all your clothes and put all found money into your "piggy bank." Cash it in. This starts money circulating.

12. List any and all monies owed to you and take one action toward getting paid back.

13. Make a list of your skills. All of them. (I can repair things in the house; I can play a few songs on guitar; I speak Spanish; I have a college degree, a high school diploma; I can read and write; I can sing on key; I am a good parent.) These are the seeds of gratitude.

14. Make an inventory of any items you might be willing to sell (not hobby supplies such as musical instruments, painting easel, tool box). Asset management.

15. Think back to how you answered the questions earlier in the "types" section of the book. How many yes answers?

16. Inventory your debts. Takes away the bogeyman and helps end vagueness.

17. Inventory your assets. Helps end vagueness.

18. List the times you have capsized success. Another early warning system.

19. List the ways you start to "act out" when you become successful or excited. Early warning again.

20. List the "warnings" friends always give you.

21. Do you feel you have a pattern of self-sabotage? Write about this.

22. What is your favorite rationalization for ruining something good? (Julia's was feeling unappreciated. Mark's was feeling bored.)

23. List things you *love* to do.

24. List 10 ways you are stingy.

25. List 10 ways you are silly (extravagant).

26. List 10 things you would like to do but haven't done.

27. Complete this sentence differently five times: If I had unlimited time and money I would _____.

28. What have you learned about yourself?

29. Use this notebook each day for any thought or feelings you might have. Do it for the rest of the 90 days.

# THE BOTTOM LINE: THE RECOVERY OF BALANCE

Sounds properly financial, doesn't it? The bottom line. Wall Street. Cash. Equity. The hard line. The line between the haves and have-nots. The bottom. The place where anything seems reasonable. Financial terms begin to swirl around in our minds.

Wrong. The bottom line as we use it refers to setting our limits in black and white. What we *won't* do goes on the line. Write a check with no money in the bank? "No. That's on my bottom line."

This phrase, as we use it, comes not from Wall Street but from one of the twelve-step fellowships, where recovering addicts set down on paper a list of behaviors that they promise they will no longer engage in.

One bottom line might look like:

1. No "kiting" checks. ("Kiting" means writing checks before the funds are in your account.)

**2.** No borrowing from the boss.

**3.** No using credit cards.

**4.** No asking friends or family for loans.

In other words, take a sheet of paper right now, get a pen, and do this: Sit quietly for a minute and take three deep breaths. In and out, in and out, in and out. Get centered and quiet enough to listen to your own "still, small voice." This voice will guide you in setting your bottom line. Everyone's bottom line is uniquely theirs. Each of us knows which behaviors make us feel shabby.

Now take the pen and write down all the behaviors that have affected you around money:

- Borrowing from lovers.
- Not balancing my checkbook.
- Using my ATM card and not recording it.
- Not keeping track of my expenditures.
- Not paying my taxes.
- Not working hard enough.

Oops. Look at that last one. Not working hard enough. That is the kind of entry we don't want. It is subjective and negative. Even though for some of us it may be true, or we may think it is true, it works better if we limit our list to the actual behaviors involving money.

For instance, instead of "Not working hard enough," we could substitute "Spending more to live than I make." This is not a judgment. It is just a fact—a fact you can now change.

As a Cash Co-Dependent, Janet's bottom line centered on behaviors that placed the financial welfare of others before her own.

- No more picking up more than my fair share of the check.
- No more buying nicer presents for friends than things for myself.
- No more loans to friends and lovers.
- No more covering more than my share of household bills without calling it an official debt, recording it, and expecting payment.
- No more tapping out my savings for family and friends.

For the Big Deal Chaser, a bottom line might entail very different behaviors. Patrick's bottom line was:

- No more working on "the big deal" instead of the job I'm being paid to do.
- No more conversations at work about big deals in the offing.
- No more using the facilities of my current job to support chasing a big deal elsewhere.
- No more spending the big deal before it's earned.
- No more living above my means, in cash.

In order to work, your bottom line must be *your* bottom line. Making a list of your unwanted behaviors pinpoints *your* problems specifically.

A Poverty Addict's bottom line might be:

- No more self-deprivation in the name of virtue.
- No more delayed self-nurturing.
- No more undercharging for services.
- No more overpayment of others.
- No more secondhand/second-best clothing, furniture, or food.

Keeping the self-criticism to a minimum, go through the process of setting a bottom line in the activities below and then try to stick to it.

Having a bottom line is a way to make ourselves feel safe. We know in black and white what we can and cannot do. We don't have to decide anew each time. And every time we stick to it, keeping this promise to ourselves makes us feel great.

---

**ACTIVITIES**

**1.** Make a list of the behaviors around money that have made you feel ashamed (e.g., bouncing checks, borrowing from friends, losing credit cards, not buying gifts for special occasions, always paying phone or electric bills at the last second, being unable to ask for a raise). Use the inventory from Week Three for help.

**2.** What other behaviors have caused you problems or made you angry at yourself or others?

**3.** Which of the behaviors above would you never want to do again, if you could help it? List these. This list is your bottom line.

**4.** Carry a copy of your bottom line with you during the remaining part of the program to remind you not to cross it.

# THE MONEY MAP: THE RECOVERY OF ACCURACY

The money map is a financial overview (or map) created by tabulating our daily expenditures into weekly totals and then adding those up into monthly totals. (In Debtors Anonymous they use something similar called a spending plan.)

Working this way through our monthly spending is like playing an elaborate game of "finders keepers." We find the money we are misspending and we learn to keep it where we'd enjoy spending it.

One of the first fruits of counting is a working knowledge of where our money goes. For most of us, this is new information. As practicing money drunks, we often feel deprived, no matter how much money we are making.

Mark discovered he spent $400 a month on diners and very little on good food. He realized that the diners he frequented never even had green vegetables. This taught him how little he cared for himself. He began to buy groceries, make breakfast and dinner, and saved $200 a month.

Julia did not have a clothing allowance for herself. She would regularly replenish her daughter's clothing but rarely her own, always finding a way to put it off till "next month." Now, she buys a couple of things a month and has new hosiery, underwear, socks, and shoes that fit. All this she bought just a little at a time, but regularly. She feels much better about herself, and dresses better, too.

As we record our expenditures for the first time, we begin to see that very often, we compulsively overspend on areas that do not count for much with us (magazines, snack foods, diners) and underspend on areas that do matter. Our flood and our drought areas stand out in stark relief. Working with our cash flow, we learn where it is impeded, where it stagnates, slows to a trickle, stops entirely, or flows freely.

Working with our daily cash counting, we can view our life as having many tributaries, like a river, into which our money flows:

| | |
|---|---|
| rent | utilities |
| household sundries | phone |
| diners/restaurants | groceries |
| entertainment | cabs |
| subways/trains | car insurance |
| car payments | gas |
| medical bills | dentist bills |
| prescriptions | clothes |
| work clothes | kids' clothes |

It is important to be accurate in our daily accounts because we will use them in making our weekly money map. The money map tells us what we spend and where we spend it.

Make a copy of the following chart to tally all your spending by category for the week (e.g., groceries—$35.76, light bill—$59.67). Use the sample chart as a guide.

| MONEY MAP | WEEK 1 | WEEK 2 | WEEK 3 | WEEK 4 | TOTAL |
|---|---|---|---|---|---|
| Net Income | | | | | |
| Rent (or Mortgage) | | | | | |
| Utilities | | | | | |
| Phone | | | | | |
| Car Insurance | | | | | |
| Rental Insurance | | | | | |
| Car Payment | | | | | |
| Gas | | | | | |
| Groceries | | | | | |
| Restaurants | | | | | |
| Tips | | | | | |
| Entertainment | | | | | |
| Health & Beauty | | | | | |
| Medical | | | | | |
| Dental | | | | | |
| Optical | | | | | |
| Veterinarian | | | | | |
| Clothing | | | | | |
| Housewares | | | | | |
| Subscriptions | | | | | |
| Books | | | | | |
| Travel/Vacation | | | | | |
| Savings | | | | | |
| Cabs/Transportation | | | | | |
| Gifts | | | | | |
| Debt Repayment | | | | | |
| Hobbies | | | | | |
| Postage | | | | | |
| Office Supplies | | | | | |
| Miscellaneous | | | | | |
| **Totals:** | | | | | |

| MONEY MAP | WEEK 1 | WEEK 2 | WEEK 3 | WEEK 4 | TOTAL |
|---|---|---|---|---|---|
| Net Income | (518) | (466) | (466) | (414) | (1864) |
| Rent (or Mortgage) | 375. | — | — | — | 375 |
| Utilities | 45. | — | — | — | 45 |
| Phone | 145. | — | — | — | 145 |
| Car Insurance | — | — | — | — | — |
| Rental Insurance | — | — | — | — | — |
| Car Payment | — | — | — | — | — |
| Gas | 19. | — | — | — | 19. |
| Groceries | 85. | 97. | 110. | 75. | 367. |
| Restaurants | 90 | 115. | 80. | 145. | 430. |
| Tips | 22. | 28. | 17. | 13. | 80. |
| Entertainment | 12 | — | 40. | 12. | 64. |
| Health & Beauty | — | 15 | 14. | — | 29 |
| Medical | — | — | — | — | — |
| Dental | — | — | — | — | — |
| Optical | 15.5 | — | — | — | 15.5 |
| Veterinarian | — | — | — | — | — |
| Clothing | — | 19 | — | 24 | 43. |
| Housewares | — | — | — | — | — |
| Subscriptions | 12. | — | — | — | 12. |
| Books | — | 15 | — | — | 15. |
| Travel/Vacation | — | — | — | — | — |
| Savings | — | — | — | — | — |
| Cabs/Transport. | 65. | 24. | 24. | 45. | 158. |
| Gifts | 30 | — | — | — | 30. |
| Debt Repayment | — | — | — | — | — |
| Miscellaneous | 45. | 35. | 64. | 37. | 181. |
| Hobbies | — | — | — | — | — |
| Postage | 10. | — | — | — | 10 |
| Office Supplies | — | — | — | — | — |
| **Totals:** | **970.5** | **348.** | **349.** | **351.** | **2018.5** |

All we want to do here is get a sense of how much it really costs us to live week to week. Most people vastly underestimate the many little costs of running a household such as groceries and clothing and utilities and then run into the red when they haven't planned for them properly. The money map is a tool to teach us exactly where we stand so that we might begin to move things around, alter the money flow to bring refreshing water to parts that are parched and dam up areas where we are losing precious water.

(One very good way to do the money map is to set aside a time at the end of each week to sit down and add up all the counting and place it into proper columns. This can be very aggravating at first as it brings up old fears and resentments, but you will feel good when it is finished. Couples should beware of this as a volatile subject but if you can remember to approach it in a spirit of love and commitment it will be highly worthwhile.)

The Money Map above is only an example. Do not use differences from your situation or income level to dismiss yourself from the program. We could have used examples ranging from many thousands a week to a couple of hundred but the amount doesn't matter. Some of us need to work on increasing our income, while others find that once their addictive mismanagement is curbed, their income is already adequate.

The above money map is from Calvin, one of our students who is a carpenter. He makes $14 an hour and works 40–50 hours a week. He nets about 74% of this figure after taxes. As you can see, Calvin has made $154.5 less money than he spent. He borrowed ahead on his paycheck to cover it. In Week Nine of the 90-day program (The Prosperity Plan), we will examine how Calvin could improve his financial situation by playing finders keepers with the money he already makes.

# THE RESOURCE LIST: THE RECOVERY OF HUMILITY

Often our families and friends are as sick as—or sicker than—us in their attitudes about money. (Like alcoholism, the addiction to money appears to run in families.) Because of this, talking to our families may not give us the support we need. Too often, they have their own denial to protect.

One of the greatest paradoxes found in early recovery is that as we break through our own denial we often find ourselves surrounded by the denial of others.

"I am a money drunk," we may confess to someone who just last week, so we'd heard, was saying exactly that about us. That very someone who had diagnosed us as money drunk may suddenly be heard to sputter, "No! I don't know if you're really *that* bad."

Even people who know us may judge us and can in fact be very shaming about our money troubles. And then, when we acknowledge it, the exchange goes something like this:

"Yes. I have realized I have a money problem. I have decided to attend a support group."

"Oh, come on! Don't go overboard! You're not as bad as Jerry, everybody has money problems. Even I myself. . . ." Denial feeds off denial.

Another person's denial is the siren's song for us, but we're alert. We know the trick here: agree with them and it's a short hop to more financial unmanageability and more self-hatred. So, instead of getting off the hook we admit: "Mine's a real problem. If you've got one, too, we could talk about it or maybe go to a support group meeting."

"Well. Mine's not *that* bad . . . heh, heh," they may answer.

And maybe it isn't that bad. *For them.*

A support group can help to make self-honesty possible. Without such help, denial may close back in again, like fog obscuring our emotional landscape. This happens because denial is chronic and because denial is catching. Once we begin to master our own, we may still get reinfected from the denial of those around us.

As newly recovering money drunks, we *do* hear symptoms of the illness everywhere, perhaps because it is epidemic, or perhaps because we begin really listening. It is, however, also true that ours is a money-drunk society. We are saturated in an ethic of materialism and overconsumption that makes our own spending patterns difficult to diagnose with clarity. The failure of our own government (the budget deficit) and financial institutions (such as the savings and loans) to act soberly illustrates the tremendous cost of group attitudes about money.

Like the alcoholic surrounded by drinkers, some social and some not, we often find ourselves watching other people's spending and taking the focus off our own. "He's worse than I am!" we say. "Why isn't he in recovery?" we may fume. For these reasons, our recovery requires support, not just insight.

It is often noted in alcoholism treatment that a person can "know" he has a drinking problem and still be unable to stop drinking based on that knowledge. We have found the same to be true of money drunks. If self-knowledge were all it took to recover, many of us would be sane, solvent, and happy instead of still struggling in the tentacles of our money problems.

Like alcoholism, the money addiction is a cunning adversary. It is adroit at disguising itself to slip through our defenses. It will tell us over and over, in any number of ways, that a debt is not a debt but a "necessary" expenditure. And of course, Madison Avenue spends billions each year to convince us this is true.

As we struggle to attain and maintain clarity about our finances, we have found that the ear and eye of a fellow recovering money drunk is a terrific support. It's the old "takes one to know one" adage in action.

In order to evaluate our new life responses, a support group is an invaluable source of mirroring.

"Am I crazy or was this crazy?" we can ask in our fellowship circles. There we can find the hope, the validation, and the nonjudgmental objectivity that can move us further into recovery.

For many of us, our first discussion with a recovering money drunk who has been in recovery for a while will feel like a revelation. "So there is hope!" we may exult.

Feeling hopeful, we may also begin to feel very, very angry as we begin the classic grieving process that is withdrawal. This hope and this sudden anger will be understandable to another recovering money drunk. This understanding may move us deeply. We may feel for the first time that we are meeting with a kindred spirit.

Meeting a recovering money drunk may feel like a godsend. It is.

## ACTIVITIES

**1.** Call Alcoholics Anonymous and find an open meeting to attend. You do not have to be an alcoholic to attend an open meeting, and you will learn a bit about how support groups work.

**2.** Look up Debtors Anonymous in your phonebook or information. Call them to see if they have meetings in your town. If so, go to one. If they don't have meetings in your town, write them a note requesting information at their New York address given below.

**3.** Reread the types of money drunks listed in this book and list any similar traits you may share with any of them.

**4.** Reread the sections on "The Way Out" at the end of each of the "types" chapters. Do they make more sense to you now?

**5.** Find out if your church or synagogue has any counseling services for money troubles. If so, go see them.

**6.** If unable to find support groups that fit your needs, use this book to start one of your own. Canvass your family and friends until you find someone else who wants to work on money. Assure them that what they tell you will be treated as confidential. You are there to help each other, not judge each other. We suggest that you meet at least once a week, opening your meeting with an assurance of anonymity. "Who you see here, what you hear here, let it stay here." Then use this book to work the 90-day program together. Use the guidelines in the money buddy chapter (Week Seven of the 90-Day Plan) to keep the emphasis on support and not criticism. Healing is an act of the soul, not the intellect. (The 12-step fellowships all have guidelines for starting and running a meeting. Adopt any one that suits your needs.)

**7.** Follow up on at least one of these possible resources; the resources below should give you a solid place to start looking for assistance to overcome the money addiction.

1. Debtors Anonymous
   General Service Board
   P.O. Box 20322
   New York, NY 10025-9992

Debtors Anonymous is growing rapidly. Strong fellowships exist in New York, California, Washington, D.C., Chicago, Los Angeles, and many other cities. Many cities now offer meetings and phone lines that are listed under the name Debtors Anonymous.

Two nonprofit organizations that have offices around the country are:

2. The National Foundation For Consumer Credit
   8701 Georgia Avenue
   Silver Spring, MD 20910
   (301) 589-5600

3. Family Service America
   Communications Department
   11700 West Lake Park Drive
   Milwaukee, WI 53224

When writing any of these groups, please enclose a self-addressed, stamped envelope so that they may respond quickly.

4. The United Way
      The United Way provides counseling centers and referrals in most cities, and can be reached by simply calling the local office of The United Way.

Also, local churches and synagogues often offer meeting places for 12-step programs such as Debtors Anonymous and/or function as clearinghouses for other helpful information.

5. Local Hospitals
      Most hospitals offer referrals for addictions counseling.

# THE MONEY BUDDY: THE RECOVERY OF TRUST

Ironically, one of the most powerful ways to shatter our denial and to move into a more healthy realism in our lives is to begin the practice of telling an intimate *exactly* what is going on with our money situation. (This is more difficult than you might at first imagine, as trust is difficult for many of us.) This chapter will help you practice how.

"No one wants to hear my troubles," is a common denial mechanism. In recovery, we learn to ask. "Who cares whether *they* want to hear it? *We* need to say it." We need to tell someone, someone we trust, to end our secrets and our shame. And to give us much-needed encouragement and even help us brainstorm solutions. (One of the things we have found very helpful is to have our money buddies come over and just sit and do their money map while we do ours.)

"How else can I know what I really think until I hear me say it," one recovering money drunk is found of saying. And, in truth we are often amazed at what comes out of our mouths— but "come out" it must. We have to be able to "name it and claim it" in order to disclaim it and change it.

Since all addictions become diseases of loneliness and isolation, and the money addiction is no different, it is important to find a "money buddy." A money buddy is someone to whom you can tell all the gory details of your money situation, someone who will be available to advise you on your money map and other recovery steps. (Often a money buddy is an invaluable ally, objectively pointing out your progress, and how well you are doing.) This person should be someone you can be honest with and not someone who will judge you. Preferably, it is someone who has some knowledge of fiscal responsibility and even recovery from the money addiction if possible.

In Debtors Anonymous, or any of the 12-step programs, this person might be called a sponsor. Regardless of what you call it, regardless of whether you seek your help through a 12-step program or independently, it will be someone to whom you can turn for advice and support.

Above all, remember to choose someone with whom you can be totally honest. The money buddy can be essential to helping you build an accurate money map and a prosperous-feeling prosperity plan.

The money buddy will not condemn your character or your past actions, or look down on you for your situation. Neither will he or she condone irresponsibility, treating you like an invalid. We are not looking for pity, sympathy, or abuse. And we are certainly not seeking out a Pollyanna who will pat our hands and say it will be all right. We are looking for a partner in planning and taking actions.

It is appropriate here to add to our caution from the previous week about families. Besides their ongoing denial, their anger can also ambush us unexpectedly in recovery. Many of us did anger our families deeply, and they may not want to see us having "too much fun" if they are still smarting, or even smirking, over our misdeeds in the past.

"Gee, it's too bad your class fell through," a family member may say, clearly delighted. "Maybe you weren't meant to take it. Maybe you should find another part-time job, instead. . . ."

It is our belief that maybe you should find another recovering money drunk, someone who wants to see you happy now, not remorseful.

The money buddy should also be able to look finances right in the eye. Look for someone who is solvent and truly cares that you get on your feet. You may want to rely on a counselor, a good friend, a pastor, a rabbi, or your spouse, anyone you think really wants you to make it—and will help you make it through your own actions.

Once your have your money buddy in place, you are now in a position to tackle another form of communication that for many of us has been both frightening and rewarding. We are referring, of course, to communication with your creditors. This communication is critical for a successful recovery but must be undertaken with great care. In order to do it effectively, it is imperative that we feel safe. To feel safe, we may need both the emotional support of a money buddy and the financial support of *savings*, which we will begin in Week Eight, The Freedom Accounts.

---

**ACTIVITIES**

**1.** Make a list of trusted nonjudgmental people. Call one up and have them come over to talk about money. Begin to disclose your true financial status.

**2.** Talk to your spouse, lover, or best friend about this process. Ask him or her to be supportive. (No, you do not need an opinion, just an ear.)

**3.** Find and read the 12-step literature (Alcoholics Anonymous, Overeaters Anonymous, Sex and Love Addicts Anonymous, for example) on sponsorship. This will help you define clear boundaries in your money-buddy pact. (See our referrals in the bibliography.)

**4.** Ask your friends how *they* handle their money. the point is that we are going to break the taboo about discussing money.

**5.** Take some time to be by yourself. Listen to your own small inner voice. Who does it say you should choose to be your money buddy? Choosing this someone is not carved in stone—you may always change it later—but choosing one helps us begin to trust our own judgments.

# THE FREEDOM ACCOUNTS: THE RECOVERY OF CHARACTER

The freedom accounts are based on two very solid premises: one, that we need savings in order to feel safe; and two, that we need to pay our debts in order to feel proud. These two truths, more than any other, guide us in building our self-esteem. And what we call "The Freedom Accounts" help us do just that.

## SAVINGS

Ten percent of whatever we make should be held aside for the future. Believe it or not, this adds up quickly, and just a few weeks of saving can be a great help in an emergency. This is the most important account we have. If you want to feel wealthy you must make more each month than you spend. It becomes a real pleasure to try to widen that gap between money earned and money spent so we can build a solid foundation of savings.

Mark had been recording his money and practicing abstinence for several months. He had also started putting aside 10 percent of his income, and even though he was making over $3,000 a month, saving $300 a month was almost impossible—in fact, at first he averaged about $200 (progress, not perfection).

It is true for many of us in early money recovery that the more we make, the more we spend. But Mark struggled to do it. He took Amtrak instead of planes, stopped eating out so much, found new ways to entertain himself, and finally was regularly saving close to 10 percent of his income. He was very happy watching his savings grow and for the first time felt like he was getting to be a "grown-up."

Then suddenly, something unexpected happened—he lost his job. The little he had been able to save over the previous months was just enough to see him through until his next job started. It was the first time in his adult life that Mark had any savings to use during an emergency. He felt solid. "I didn't have to borrow from anyone to get by—it was great."

We cannot state strongly enough that the commitment to save even 10 percent is an investment in self-worth that you cannot skip safely. As a rule of thumb, savings equal to three months' pay is a goal worth shooting for. While building that, any savings at all builds a sense of security that is greater than the actual monies entailed.

## DEBT REPAYMENT

Solvency is balance in our lives as a whole. Once we have gained stability by starting abstinence, asking for help, and building a savings account, we can begin to start repaying our debts. This is an absolute must in order to wipe the slate clean and clear our conscience of any past abuses.

Before Mark hit his financial bottom, he was in debt to various friends and institutions who had supported him in his development of his radio devices. When the overseas merchandising failure sent him into bankruptcy, and he faced up to his money addiction, he took a big deal approach to paying everyone back, figuring something "big" would happen that would allow him to pay everyone back all at once.

Oddly enough, at that moment, a major department store chain called and asked him to demonstrate his radio for them. They took him to lunch and told him about all the millionaires they had made of young men just like him. Instead of beginning debt repayment, he got all excited and knew for certain that this was his lucky break. He spent all his money he made from his day job to build a prototype radio to show them. They liked what they saw and gave him a little money to test it in a town not far from his. He *borrowed* a friend's car, *borrowed* money for his design engineers, *borrowed* money for his trip, and away he went.

He got to shake the chairman's hand, but he never got anything like the millions promised over lunch. Further in debt than ever, Mark in turn promised his friends again that he would indeed pay them.

He lost friends and credibility.

He learned his lesson.

It is up to you how you pay people. Most of our students pay the most important debts first: late rent, car payments, utility bills. It is important that you take care of yourself first. If you lose your house, your car, your health, you won't be able to pay anyone anyway.

Some recovering money drunks pay people back based on their need. For Mark, some of his friends had come to need the money badly, so he paid them first. Some who were more well off received token payments or phone calls with a commitment to full future repayment.

Some people make a list of all their debts and then divide the sum of each individual debt by the total number of dollars they owe. Then each person gets a monthly percentage of the total indebtedness times whatever money you set aside each money for debt repayment.

For example: suppose you owe a total of $1,000. $200 to Bill, $400 to Todd, and $400 to Mary. That means 40 percent of your debt is to Mary, 40 percent of your debt is to Todd, and 20 percent of your debt is to Bill. Suppose you can pay $50 a month to debts. Well, Todd gets 40 percent of $50, which is $20, as does Mary; and Bill gets $10, which is 20 percent of $50.

We must emphasize again that the amount you allot to debt repayment must not be so large as to jeopardize your current solvency. Retiring an old debt by acquiring a new one is not our goal. Freedom from debt is. And we use what we call the Windfall Rule for dealing with sudden infusions of cash. The rule states that when we receive money over and above our weekly salary, (for example, a tax refund, payment for a large free-lance job, winning the lottery, an inheritance) we use one-third for the past (debt repayment), one-third for the present (reward), and one-third for the future (savings). We also suggest you keep a running total of all debts paid and think of it as a Freedom Account. Each entry of debts paid brings us closer to freedom.

---

**ACTIVITIES**

**1.** List five incidences of money shame that really bother you. What are their common denominators? Share them with your money buddy. Another lesson in trust.

**2.** Separate your money behaviors from your character by listing five positive traits in yourself. Share these traits with your money buddy. A lesson in self-esteem.

**3.** List the names and addresses of all the people you owe money and set a time to contact them. No need to send payment yet, just acknowledge the debt and your intention to pay. Be careful not to set an unrealistic time frame or to make promises you won't be able to keep. (No need to spill your guts in apology or to expect them to be loving about it, just make arrangements to contact them and do it.) This may be the hardest thing you ever do, and it may take some of you a while longer to get up the courage. This is okay.

**4.** Remind yourself *you* are not your debts. Add your name to the list of debts owed. Be good to yourself.

**5.** Arrange a meeting with your money buddy to discuss a reasonable payment plan for these debts.

**6.** Send each creditor a letter saying when and how much you will pay. (Do not go overboard and promise something you cannot do. Even a letter to tell creditors that you have not forgotten the debt but cannot yet pay it will help).

**7.** What can you sell? What can you barter? Just looking at the worse-case scenario can give us peace of mind.

**8.** What small things could you do to make yourself feel prosperous? (For example, stationery with letterhead, business cards, stamps by the roll, a navy blue suit, a clean apartment, your laundry done, a full refrigerator, polished shoes, a manicure, a clean car, newly painted walls. This is a tool for self-nurturing. If looking at debts makes you feel broke, use one of your list of prosperous actions to make you feel better. Mark's is filling the refrigerator or doing all the laundry. Julia's is buying a new writing notebook.)

**9.** Fix or throw out one broken thing. Do this once a week; it will help you feel better about your life.

**10.** List 100 things you are proud of. (Yes, *100*.) Keep the list. This is to help cheer us up and remind us that we have many assets that aren't in dollars.

**11.** Make a freedom account for savings. How much can you put in regularly? Make a commitment to do it. Do it.

**12.** Make a freedom account for all debt repayment. List amount, the date, to whom it was paid, and how much is still owed. Celebrate each debt retirement. (Without debting.)

# THE PROSPERITY PLAN: THE RECOVERY OF JOY

Like the money map, this tool is grounded in the realities of our daily spending. Using our counting as a springboard, we return to our categories of cash flow. Whereas the money map showed us where our money goes and how much we use to live, this time, we try to prioritize the money flow in ways that better serve our wants and needs.

Our money map may show us that we skimp on groceries and fuel our lives with junk food from delis and diners. We redistribute these funds and eat better for less money, with a little left over for savings. This was one of the first changes Mark made in his recovery.

| Money Map | | Prosperity Plan | |
|---|---|---|---|
| Delis | $380 | Delis, diners | $200 |
| Groceries | $240 | Groceries | $380 |
| | | Savings | $40 |

Our money map may reveal that we use cabs when we could walk or use mass transit. Or that we have *no* allotment at all for entertainment. (The single most common mistake our students make is that they do not allow themselves regular entertainment. It is pretty difficult to feel good about the world if there's no fun in your life.) Workaholic money drunks can live on all work and no play and go broke taking cabs and ordering food into the office! Again, we redistribute our funds. We do this realistically. These seemingly small changes are *progress*.

| Money Map | | Prosperity Plan | |
|---|---|---|---|
| Cabs | $120 | Cabs | $20 |
| Entertainment | $0 | Transit | $40 |
| | | Entertainment | $40 |
| | | Savings | $20 |

Each prosperity plan will be different, as we all have different ways in which we mismanage our money. Some will need to put in clothing allowances, others will find they overspend on clothes they never wear. Almost all of us will find we have not been saving enough money to make us feel safe. To feel prosperous you need to make more money than you spend, so savings is a number-one priority.

The money buddy is extremely helpful when we make a prosperity plan. He or she can be the conscience of our solvency. Are we realistic in our wants, in our expectations; are we taking care of ourselves first? These are important questions of balance that the money buddy can provide.

Remember the money map is the actual spending that we do, and the prosperity plan is our goal. We compare these two sets of numbers monthly until, over time, the prosperity plan and the money map converge. When our plans match our earning and spending, our lives will have progressed a great deal toward our goal: safe, solvent, and happy.

The prosperity plan is a tool aimed at minimizing our sense

of deprivation. We begin to see that even without significantly increasing our financial cash flow we can increase our sense of financial well-being. We learn that *how* we spend matters nearly as much as how much we *have* to spend. For most money drunks, this is very important information. Prosperity planning, even in early recovery, maybe especially in early recovery, creates a sense of self-worth. It's important to remember—*self-worth always grows from self-care.*

We money drunks are often extremists. Once we realize the pain our financial unmanageability has caused others we are *extremely* sorry; so sorry that we can sabotage our own recovery by donning sackcloth and ashes and living out an unlivable austerity as penance for our problematic pasts.

Focused on our debts to others, we forget our debts to our-selves. Designing a prosperity plan that allocates our current funds into spending categories, we often overspend on debt re-payments, making up to others by making do ourselves. This is a good time to remember charity begins at home—and really be-gin it there, with yourself.

Any recovery based on self-punishment leads us straight to self-sabotage. Any present that focuses obsessively on our past dooms us to repeat it. A daily reprieve from *destructive* spending must be based on a daily commitment to *constructive* spending, not on beating ourselves up with guilt.

It is not enough to stop spending foolishly. We must now begin spending wisely. Spending wisely means acknowledging our wants as well as our needs, our dreams as well as our obligations.

One of the things we need to do when making a prosperity plan is to learn the essence of what we want, not just the price tag. Many times things we think of as beyond our reach become available if we will get creative about how to get them.

For example, Julia needed a new car. Her car was falling

apart and when some major repairs became needed she talked it over with her money buddy and decided to look for a replacement.

He had her list in her notebook what exactly she wanted in a new vehicle. What she wanted was a four-wheel drive similar to her last one. Her money buddy pressed her, What things would you like different? She listed the essentials: stereo, four doors, air conditioning, and the same dependability. A new version of her old truck cost $18,900 plus. She test drove the new models and was about to make the purchase when her money buddy suggested she look at used trucks. She found one she loved that was the top of the line: leather interior, automatic everything, trailer hitch, the works, with a complete warranty that matched the warranty on a new car. She saved $7,900 because she learned to use her prosperity plan to ask for the essence of what she wanted, and to rely on her money buddy to remind her to "always shop around for a major purchase."

Often we think we know how much something will cost and assume that it is outside our grasp when, in reality, we might have the essence of the thing we want—if only we learn to describe what it is we like about it without getting caught up in the negativity of our disease.

Early in our recovery, we often think of God as a trickster. When our car breaks down we consider it "proof" we were wrong to earmark funds for a creative writing class. Instead of looking for a creative means to pay for both, we settle for an excuse to sabotage our joy. Grudgingly, we pay for the car, decide not to take the class, and then we pay for that choice with depression. Depression leads us into "what's the use" thinking, which leads us into "what the hell" thinking, which leads us into thinking we can buy an outfit on credit.

This spending (the "it doesn't matter and neither do I" kind) takes us further into debt but no further toward our dreams.

Without dreams, recovery is a dreary landscape and one we will not live in for very long. This is one of the reasons our attempts to dig out financially have not worked. We make the future too bleak a place for anyone to live there. We must turn our creativity toward living at least a part of our dreams right from the beginning. (It is enough if at first all you want is your rent paid and some food on the table, but this comes quickly and soon we must expand our horizons.)

Although we hide this fact from ourselves by focusing solely on the negativity and wreckage of our pasts, we money drunks are creative with our finances. We turned it toward wheeling and dealing, juggling and jiggling our finances and our stories. In recovery, we need to reharness our financial wizardry. The same ingenuity that went into borrowing money can now go into plans for innovative earning and saving.

Terese, a writing teacher, recovering from poverty addiction, swapped one of her writing seminars for singing lessons with a singing teacher who wanted to learn to write. Terese had always told herself, "Someday, when I'm rich, I'm going to learn to really sing." She's doing it now and it gives her life a feeling of abundance.

Candace, a makeup artist and recovering compulsive spender, swapped her lady lawyer a beauty make-over for some legal advice. Her lawyer got a new and lovely look. Candace got the legal help she needed without having to go into debt.

Tom, a recovering Big Deal Chaser, has started acting classes. He finds that the creativity and energy he used to make a deal can also help him to "sell" a character. Tom had always wanted to act but was always afraid of looking foolish. He chased the big deal in search of enough self-importance to allow himself to "afford" taking risks. In recovery, he has dropped his need to be perfect. As a result, he has discovered he is a pretty darn good actor. (And it's fun.)

There are many ways to skin the proverbial cat. Brainstorm a little and see if you can't lead a richer and more expanded life with a little creativity instead of a lot of cash.

We mean that if the car breaks down and takes your extra money you were planning to spend on a class and you still want to take that class, see if you can barter something, swap your skills for another person's skills. Maybe your mechanic would like your help designing an ad for his business even more than he would like the cash for fixing your clunker. It can't hurt to ask.

## MAKING A PROSPERITY PLAN

To make a prosperity plan we need three things: a job (or steady legal income from somewhere such as child support), a money map, and a money buddy who will look it over when we are done.

The job is the first thing we need because we must have some money coming in to work with, no matter how little. Believe it or not, many of us have gotten by so long on big deal chasing and borrowing from friends or family or just plain doing without, that a job, any kind of job, is necessary for self-reliance as well as self-esteem.

There is a famous story in AA of Bobby E., who, when he first got sober, was living in an abandoned car and living off the streets. Within his first few days of sobriety he asked his sponsor what he should do and the sponsor said, "Get a job." To this Bobby replied, "I'm living in an abandoned car, I have no teeth, I look terrible." To which his sponsor replied, "So get a terrible job." The rest of the story is famous because Bobby did exactly that and within a few years was a wealthy man.

So, first get a job. Any kind of job. (If you have one already—congratulate yourself.)

Second, write down a month's spending so that you have a map of where your money goes. (Most of you will have done that by now.)

Third, ask your money buddy to oversee your plan and make a date to meet with him or her to discuss it. (Setting a time will motivate you to make the plan.)

Fill out the categories of your prosperity plan with the monthly totals from your money map. These entries become the Actual column, meaning that this is what you actually spent last month. Then you examine each expenditure to see where you might be able to use your money more effectively. This is where your "still, small voice," can be very helpful. And when you are finished filling in the categories and deciding how you would like to change your spending habits, you call in your money buddy, show him or her the changes, and ask for an opinion. (It is here that you will learn the competency level of your money buddy.)

This is the first attempt on the road to considered spending that is the true path to solvency and joy. First, we need safety and a sense of being in control of our finances by saving and planning each purchase. This comfort lays the groundwork from which we will begin to uncover our dreams, and the focus of our battle will change from desperation to one of living in personal fulfillment.

A. Looking at his money map we can see that Calvin could save $45 a month by cutting down on his long distance phone bills.

B. He could improve his standard of living by buying better groceries and cooking at home.

C. Calvin could save $230 a month by cutting out his fast food dining.

D. Less restaurant meals mean Calvin is less tempted to over tip his friendly waitress.

E. If Calvin wants to enjoy his life now instead of later he could find another $86 a month for entertainment.

| PROSPERITY PLAN | PLAN | ACTUAL | DIFFERENCE | ACTION |
|---|---|---|---|---|
| Net Income | | | | |
| Rent (or Mortgage) | | | | |
| Utilities | | | | |
| Phone | | | | |
| Car Insurance | | | | |
| Rental Insurance | | | | |
| Car Payment | | | | |
| Gas | | | | |
| Groceries | | | | |
| Restaurants | | | | |
| Tips | | | | |
| Entertainment | | | | |
| Health & Beauty | | | | |
| Medical | | | | |
| Dental | | | | |
| Optical | | | | |
| Veterinarian | | | | |
| Clothing | | | | |
| Housewares | | | | |
| Subscriptions | | | | |
| Books | | | | |
| Travel/Vacation | | | | |
| Savings | | | | |
| Cabs/Transportation | | | | |
| Gifts | | | | |
| Debt Repayment | | | | |
| Hobbies | | | | |
| Postage | | | | |
| Office Supplies | | | | |
| Miscellaneous | | | | |
| **Totals** | | | | |

| PROPERITY PLAN | PLAN | ACTUAL | DIFFER | COMMENTS |
|---|---|---|---|---|
| Net Income | (1864) | (1864) | | |
| Rent (or Mortgage) | 375 | 375 | 0 | |
| Utilities | 45 | 45 | 0 | |
| Phone | 100 | 145 | −45 | A. |
| Car Insurance | — | — | — | |
| Rental Insurance | — | — | — | |
| Car Payment | — | — | — | |
| Gas | 19 | 19 | 0 | |
| Groceries | 400 | 367 | +33 | B. |
| Restaurants | 200 | 430 | −230 | C. |
| Tips | 40 | 80 | −40 | D. |
| Entertainment | 150 | 64 | +86 | E. |
| Health & Beauty | 29 | 29 | 0 | |
| Medical | — | — | — | |
| Dental | — | — | — | |
| Optical | 16 | 15.5 | +5 | F. |
| Veterinarian | — | — | — | |
| Clothing | 50 | 43 | +7 | G. |
| Housewares | — | — | — | |
| Subscriptions | 12 | 12 | 0 | |
| Books | 10 | 15 | −5 | H. |
| Travel/Vacation | — | — | — | |
| Savings | 235 | 0 | +235 | I. |
| Cabs/Transportation | 80 | 158 | −78 | J. |
| Gifts | 50 | 30 | +20 | K. |
| Debt Repayment | — | — | — | |
| Hobbies | — | — | — | |
| Postage | 10 | 10 | 0 | |
| Office Supplies | — | — | — | |
| Miscellaneous | 43 | 181 | −138 | L. |
| **Totals** | 1864 | 2018.5 | −154.5 | M. |

F. Calvin wears contacts and this money is for maintenance.

G. We doubt whether Calvin is adequately clothed because he obviously is buying clothes only when he needs them. A more realistic clothing allowance will show itself over time by doing the money maps.

H. Not bad. Pretty close to plan. He might even want to up his allocation for books.

I. Calvin should immediately plan some savings. He has medical and dental insurance on his job but none of his paycheck saved should he get sick. No rainy day money.

J. Again, he could save quite a bit of money by not taking cabs to the job site.

K. Calvin counts his expenditures on gifts, in this case it was for flowers for a friend.

L. Calvin could keep better track of his money and then he would be able to either cut these expenses or move them into proper categories. (This is very common when we first start counting our money.)

M. As we can see, with just a small amount of changes, Calvin can eat better, have more fun, and begin to build himself a freedom account without having to borrow ahead on his paycheck.

Some of us will be similar to Calvin and be making just enough to make ends meet, some of us will have many thousands more in income and still need to spend our time and money more wisely, and many of us will have many debts hanging over our heads that we need to pay. Use your prosperity plan to help you set a reasonable debt repayment schedule based on your ability to pay.

## ACTIVITIES

Note: We want you to do the following exercises in order to get in touch with just how many options you have and how much there is to do and appreciate in your life. This helps overcome feelings of entrapment and boredom essential to recovering joyfulness in our lives. Remember: There is no monetary equivalent for joy.

**1.** List five fields of study that interest you.

**2.** Select one topic and start a "clip file" on it.

**3.** Make yourself an "ideas" folder. File all brainstorms.

**4.** List five "other lives" you think you'd enjoy, for example, doctor, lawyer, Indian chief, belly dancer, astronaut.

**5.** In the life you've got right now, select one piece of "play" related to one of your "other" lives. Allow yourself to play it (such as taking a belly dancing class).

**6.** What more are you learning about yourself? Make a list of 10 insights. Share them with your money buddy.

**7.** What good qualities do you have? Add 10 of them to your list. Share these with your money buddy.

**8.** What values are important to you? Put 10 of them on the list. Share these with your money buddy.

**9.** Choose to let go of desperation. Write in your journal about it.

**10.** Visualize yourself with everything you need. What is it? Write it down.

**11.** Fix all broken household items. Okay, fix one.

**12.** Sell or give away five things you don't want.

**13.** List 20 things you like to do (and the last time you did them). How much does each cost?

**14.** List 20 things you can do for under $20. Do one a week.

**15.** Complete this sentence differently five times: Rich people like to _____ (go to dinner, ride horses, go dancing, go to the theater . . .). Make plans to do one of these in order to foster a sense of fun.

# THE TIME GRID: THE RECOVERY OF SELF

For most of us, the valuable commodity of time is one we spend thoughtlessly or allow others to spend for us. Our jobs get a lot of it; our co-workers get a lot of it. We spend time chatting and not really working. Or we listen to friends over and over when we are on deadline and spreading ourselves too thin, which means we overwork and usually underaccomplish.

The same is true with our leisure hours. We go to the gym and socialize instead of work out. Then we're mad we "don't have time" to really get in shape.

In short, we often overcommit to others—and undercommit to ourselves.

No time to exercise.

No time for the friends we'd really like to see, always having to cancel entertainment with friends due to "work." No time for family except "on the fly."

No time to think about any of this and fix it.

Keeping track of your time will show you how much time

you use on passive entertainments, like TV, or bar-hopping, or dining. But the most important thing we usually learn is just how much or how little time we ourselves *control*.

*So take some time to do this*. We've done some of the legwork for you . . . .

Of the many books on time, one stands out as exceptionally useful. It is *Organizing for Work*, by H. L. Gantt, published in 1930! From that book, we have adapted a tool that we call "the Time Grid." (We'd like to thank Dr. Sheila Flaherty-Jones for her help with this.) Our grid is really an offshoot of what is known in logistics planning as a Gantt chart, or in many graduate schools as critical path analysis. (The grid is simpler for our needs.)

Essentially, the Gantt chart was developed for moving men and materials against a deadline in order to bring a job in on time. A true Gantt chart starts backward from the due date and measures what has to be completed in order to do each successive part of a project. Often our money addiction has kept us off balance for so long that we don't really manage our time efficiently. Working with the grid will give us a sense of how we spend it, and, more important, the grid will help us spend it to best advantage.

This method of breaking down a project will work no matter what the goal is. Want to lose 20 pounds? One pound a week for 20 weeks will do it. Want to learn to paint? One hour a day times six months will be 180 hours' worth of painting practice. Plant a garden? Work on your car? Sew some curtains? Remodel the house? Learn to play the piano? (Keep the emphasis on "play.") One hour a day times six months becomes 180 hours of "play.")

A foreign language—same idea. Make a feature film, crossing the Alps.

The amazing thing about the time grid is that we all can find that one hour. No matter how hard we work or how hard we play. It's just an hour. One day at a time. It is okay to pile three hours up in one day; that can work just as well. But the important thing is that we schedule it in for ourselves and then follow through.

The grid symbolizes our commitment and it protects us from wanted (and unwanted) intrusions on our new goals.

"Can you talk for a while?"

"No, dear, not right now, I have class."

"Could you . . . run to the hardware store with me to get that paint? . . . run lines with me? . . . move the living room couch? . . ."

"No, I'm afraid I have to practice. Give me an hour."

The grid protects us and sees us through. It helps remove the anxiety that choice can produce. Without the grid, it is often a dilemma about what we are going to do next. (We feel we "should" do so many things and wish we "could" do so many more.) The grid removes that confusion. The grid keeps us calm; we just put one foot in front of the other.

Do the right thing. And it's right there in black and white. The grid also keeps us focused on what we are doing. At work, I work. (I'll do my homework at home). This way I don't steal time from my boss. This way I don't "stress out."

At peak performance, we have peak stress. What happens is that we play or work at peak levels for too long and soon the stress causes injuries, mental lapses, fatigue, or depression. And we go into a slump.

However, if we can back ourselves down from the peak level of performance—just a bit—it can help avoid "burnout." We can play at 90 percent efficiency almost indefinitely.

The grid can help us alleviate burnout because it does away with the all-nighter approach to getting things done. The key to its success is that it is flexible and nurturing.

First, it is flexible because there will be scheduled alternatives—if I can't practice this Tuesday, then I will do it on Wednesday evening when I have another open slot.

Second, it is nurturing because the most important thing we schedule is play time, nurturing time. Two hours a day that is just ours, no matter what our deadlines are—no matter what we have to do—no matter how excited we are about a project.

*Impossible!* Two full hours for ourselves? Yes.

A class, a walk, exercise, a movie, sitting around, 14 hours a week that are for us. Depending on your perspective, 14 hours could seem like a lot or very little. The point is—it is enough.

Before you decide the grid won't work for you, work with it. Make yourself a grid by dividing a sheet of paper into seven columns (one for each day of the week). Then on the left side write the hours in a day, say, from six a.m. to midnight. (Most of us sleep from at least midnight to six.)

Now just fill in the "grid" of time with whatever your activities are: nine to five maybe is work. Maybe you take a class on Tuesday and Thursday night from six to nine. You want to play the piano—schedule in some piano time. Whatever your schedule, put it in. Now schedule time for exercise, and for entertainment; remember to fill in some times for "free" space. That is a grid.

Start filling it in. Put on it what you must and what you choose. Remember to play.

What we *become* on the grid is *consistent.* Daily play, daily work, daily study, daily prayer. *What* we become, daily and consistently, is up to us.

There is an old saying: "If you want something done, give it to the busiest person you know."

**ACTIVITIES**

**1.** Make a time grid of your current schedule. (One of the reasons we use the grid is to help us get over our sense of deprivation.)

**2.** How much time have you allotted for yourself? How much time do you feel you waste? In what ways could you change it?

**3.** Make a new grid with your changes in mind.

**4.** Post it in a couple of places.

**5.** Put something on the grid for fun. Do it.

**6.** Plan a family outing. Put it on the grid.

**7.** Go over your grid with your money buddy.

## TIME GRID

| | Sunday | Monday | Tuesday | Wednesday | Thursday | Friday | Saturday |
|---|---|---|---|---|---|---|---|
| **7 to 9** | ZZZ | Breakfast Get to Work | Breakfast Get to Work | Breakfast with friend Get to Work | Breakfast Get to Work | Breakfast Do Nails Get to Work | Breakfast Bike Ride |
| **9 to 11** | Wash Hair Do Mending | Work | Work | Work | Work | Work | Bike Ride / Laundry |
| **11 to 1** | Brunch | Work / Lunch Out | Work / Lunch at Desk | Work / Museum Bag Lunch | Work / Lunch with Friend | Work / Bookstore Bag Lunch | Laundry / Grocery Shop |
| **1 to 3** | Walk or Read | Work | Work | Work | Work | Work | Clean Apartment / Nap |
| **3 to 5** | Concert | Work | Work | Work | Work | Work | Nap / Friend Over |
| **5 to 7** | Early Dinner Out | Gym | Cook at Home | Gym / Sandwich Out | Cook At Home | Gym | Friend Over / Cook |
| **7 to 9** | Prepare Clothes for Work Week | Go to Meeting / Attend Support Group Meeting | Prepare for Thursday Class | Attend Support Group Meeting | Art History Class | Attend Support Group Meeting | Cook / Friends to Dinner |
| **9 to 11** | Prepare for Work Week | Free Time | Free Time | Free Time | Free Time | Movie Date | Free Time |
| **11 to 7** | ZZZ | ZZZ | ZZZ | ZZZ | ZZZ | ZZZ | ZZZ |

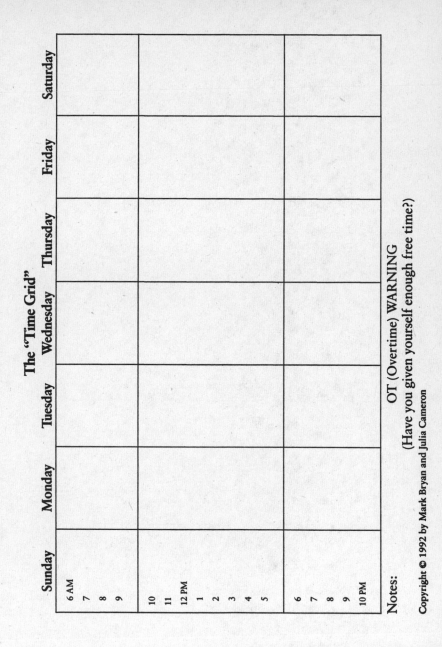

The "Time Grid"

|  | Sunday | Monday | Tuesday | Wednesday | Thursday | Friday | Saturday |
|---|---|---|---|---|---|---|---|
| 6 AM |  |  |  |  |  |  |  |
| 7 |  |  |  |  |  |  |  |
| 8 |  |  |  |  |  |  |  |
| 9 |  |  |  |  |  |  |  |
| 10 |  |  |  |  |  |  |  |
| 11 |  |  |  |  |  |  |  |
| 12 PM |  |  |  |  |  |  |  |
| 1 |  |  |  |  |  |  |  |
| 2 |  |  |  |  |  |  |  |
| 3 |  |  |  |  |  |  |  |
| 4 |  |  |  |  |  |  |  |
| 5 |  |  |  |  |  |  |  |
| 6 |  |  |  |  |  |  |  |
| 7 |  |  |  |  |  |  |  |
| 8 |  |  |  |  |  |  |  |
| 9 |  |  |  |  |  |  |  |
| 10 PM |  |  |  |  |  |  |  |

OT (Overtime) WARNING
(Have you given yourself enough free time?)

Notes:

# THE RELAPSE CHECKLIST: THE RECOVERY OF COMPASSION

For most money drunks, the journey to health is a bumpy one. We hit bottom, bounce into recovery, and bounce right out of it again until we hit a new bottom and bounce back in. We work our recovery and we fight our recovery. It is very important that we remember to be compassionate for ourselves and take each setback as a necessary step in the process toward solvency.

The admission that we spend (or scrooge) addictively is not an easy one. For most of us, the surrender is gradual and grudging. Despite our history of countless failed attempts to control and enjoy our money, we lapse easily into believing that "this time will be different" or that "more money means more manageability."

Using our primary tools, many of us achieve rapid financial gains. We stop acquiring debts. We clean up old debts. Our credit rating returns to normal. Our lives feel expansive and abundant. Then, one day, they don't anymore. We realize we have relapsed.

What happened? Usually lots of little things.

Lulled into a false sense of security, or tricked by success, we stopped counting our blessings—or our spending. We skipped our weekly tallies. We bypassed calls to our money buddy. We began to keep financial secrets again. Our mail piled up a little. We didn't balance our checkbook for a month.

Why would we do that? We'd never do that. And yet we have. Why a relapse?

There are those who would say arrogance precedes a financial relapse. This may be true in some cases. However, we have found it equally true that it is our perfectionism that trips us up and starts the downward spiral into renewed financial disaster.

Cassie, a recovering money drunk, had her purse stolen. In that purse was her wallet and the small notebook she had been using for counting.

"It was losing the notebook that threw me," she says. And where it threw her was into a relapse.

"I guess I felt 'what's the use?' I had lost my notebook. I did not immediately go to buy another, and within two days my money was 'disappearing' again. My old friend 'instant amnesia' was back and I was unable to tell you where my money went."

Cassie's "tantrum" continued for nearly a month. Such tantrums are familiar behavior to many recovering money drunks. Like alcoholics seeking an excuse to drink ("He drove me to it") we money drunks often fall from grace behind fits of pique.

"The bank made a mistake and bounced a check." So we write another bad one and blame it on them. Fragile in our self-worth, rigid in early recovery, we take mistakes, errors, and mishaps very hard. "What's the use?" we berate ourselves, and then go on to "finish the bender."

This self-destructive bingeing is a way we punish ourselves, and punish the God or "gods" that "let" it happen to us. We are like frightened children acting up by acting out.

Most of us find that our money-drunk relapses can be traced to a reawakened sense of shame. Any situation, incident, or episode that mirrors our shaky past can create a dangerous situation in which our subconscious impulse is to sabotage our recovery.

Think for a moment of all the shame we feel as practicing money drunks:

- When we bounce a check, we are ashamed.
- When our bank statement can't be reconciled, we're ashamed.
- When our credit rating falters, we're ashamed.
- When our rent is late, we're ashamed.
- When our taxes aren't paid, we're ashamed.
- When we scrimp on groceries, we're ashamed.
- When we can't repay a loan, we're ashamed.

Our shame makes us frightened. Feeling like scolded children, we are wary of all financial personnel. They are authority figures to us. This makes us hostile, belligerent, timid, flustered, anxious, irritable, obsequious, servile—anything but our best selves.

As money drunks we are often frightened by:

- any mail that looks "financial";
- any mail that looks "legal";
- any call that sounds "official";
- any notice that looks "official".

We are often aggravated, frightened, or angered by bank tellers, cashiers, the postman. We're intimidated by lawyers, even more so by accountants. The word "IRS" may set us shaking. April 15 can feel like "doomsday" to people like us.

Although some of us own homes, run businesses, practice law or medicine, teach, and very often manage other people's money, we still don't feel like adults. Carrying our guilty secrets, we feel like guilty kids—shame, shame, shame, on us!!!

## RELAPSE SYMPTOMS

Most of us experience two very different sets of relapse symptoms: one internal, one external. The internal ones are the relapses to negative thinking and the external ones are relapses to negative actions. Both usually announce themselves as one or more of the following signs:

1. Confused thinking. Spending too much time daydreaming or feeling lost in thought with an inability to focus clearly on what we are doing. Wishful thinking.

2. Difficulty in sleeping because of money worries or dread, or difficulty in staying calm during the normal course of the day.

3. Memory failure and an inability to concentrate on counting, keeping a journal, or abstinence, or other tasks.

4. Sudden bursts of emotion, crying, rage, or panic attacks. Overreacting to criticism.

5. Loss of control with physical actions leading to accidents.

6. "Doubting our sanity," with feelings of being crazy, shame, guilt, or hopelessness. Oversleeping. (This is often a sign of depression.)

7. Excessive concern for others without thoughts about ourselves.

8. Avoidance of friends and family and especially those associated with our recovery.

9. Pointing the finger at others with resentments about how we have been wronged. Becoming a victim and thinking defensively. Blaming.

10. Feelings of loneliness and desperation. A feeling that "It's too late," "I can't do this," "I'm too far gone."

11. Loss of gratitude and refusal to see the whole picture. Self-obsession without concern for right action and process.

12. Inability to make daily commitments. Refusal to attend support group meetings.

13. Apathy, discounting, and grandiosity in which we decide "I don't care," "It's not that big a deal," or "I don't need help." Refusal to start at the beginning.

14. Loss of self-care, such as counting, exercising, or making personal contact with family and friends.

15. Loss of options. We lose sight of our many choices in any situation.

16. Ego. We let our perfectionism keep us from working on our recovery because of some minor (or major) error in judgment, such as going on a spending binge, refusing to balance our checkbook, forgetting to record expenses in our journals or feeling inferior.

## LEARNING THE LANGUAGE

Shame is often reawakened by our feelings of inferiority, of being dumb, of not knowing what people mean when they talk about money. Therefore, it is imperative that we learn the basic language of finance in order to keep from being intimidated when discussing money. This knowledge helps us recover our sense of power.

There are several important concepts and techniques that we need to learn in order to be fluent in the language of merchants and others with whom we will have to deal as our financial goals are realized and we begin to fulfill our dreams, whether those dreams mean going to college, buying a new car or home, investing in stocks, or planning our retirement. Study the language of basic finance until it loses the power to intimidate you. The list of words below is a solid place to start:

stocks

FDIC

Social Security

broker

gross revenue

net revenue

tuition

savings rate

compound interest

simple interest

return on investment

net worth

liability

asset

debt service

bonds

equity

interest rate

cash flow

down payment

revolving charge

IRA

income tax

We hear these words around us every day. In order that we not be intimidated into thinking financial management is over our head it is time to learn them. Though we feel strongly that these tools will bring about a new understanding and financial composure in these 90 days, it is also important to realize that there are no quick fixes. This foothold will surely set you on the path up the mountain but you must realize that the work will be ongoing.

## RELINQUISHING RESENTMENT

As in all addictions, relapse is often preceded by a recurrent resentment. The preoccupation with other people's money can poison us. The banner headlines in the *Wall Street Journal* about the salaries made by the most elite in our field can discourage us into quitting. At the very least, it takes us out of the day we are in, and ruins our mood, bringing up feelings of anger, despair, or resentment.

For a recovering money drunk, these feelings are dangerous. They keep us from staying focused on our jobs, our families, our lives, and our blessings. Instead of rejoicing in the fact that we have jobs, we compare ourselves to the millionaires; the first acting class gets judged against Robert De Niro; the first script held up against the $1.2 million paid by a movie studio to someone else.

This focus on money and fame is a drug that deadens our senses. We feel less, think less, see less, taste less, and life even loses its sweet aroma. Often our first attempts at a new creative or business endeavor are judged against the best in the world, because that's whom we read about, listen to, watch. This practice can be devastating to our self-worth and even more damaging to our productivity. This comparison is what kills most artists.

For many money drunks, stress creates the yes to addictive spending. Angry with our spouses, our bosses, our children, hurt by friends, disappointed by the reception to a good piece of work, we are rendered needy and therefore greedy for the quick fix. A relapse is really a collapse of our defenses.

Any time our upkeep activities become erratic, we know we are in danger of relapse. Are we:

- counting? journaling? exercising?
- doing weekly money summaries?
- talking to our money buddy? Regularly?
- using our money map?
- sticking to our prosperity plan?

Very often, change creates pain. Rather than feel the pain of healthy change, we often reach back to our addiction to feel the old familiar pain instead. Relapse is a u-turn back to the familiar. Odd as it may sound, we money drunks may buy ourselves something to make ourselves feel worse, not better.

"I was afraid Jason was leaving me," says Mimi of her relapse. "I couldn't face that thought so I bought two coats I didn't need. With my cards maxed-out, I had bouncing checks to worry about instead of Jason."

Relapse comes in many forms but so does recovery. A bounced check, spending that is not on your map, a binge of junk spending—these toxic adventures pale quickly once some recovery has been experienced.

"Even when I'm not doing as well as I could," Mimi exclaims, "two coats isn't two months rent. In the old days it would have been." It is important we stay grounded in the now because our recovery takes place in the present.

Recovery involves sharing of ourselves and being vulnerable to others. We must learn to risk our hero image. This is hard to do when money has always been used to cover glaring weaknesses or deep wounds. We often must fight the feeling that we will disappear.

## AN EARLY WARNING

We want to give you an early warning. It is: Watch out for Success, the Unseen Enemy.

As money drunks, we often pride ourselves on our success at bouncing back from failure. We survive. We pick up the pieces. We move on.

What we often do not see is that there is a reason we are constantly picking ourselves up, constantly bouncing back, constantly moving on. Often the real reason we relapse is the stress caused by success.

As practicing money drunks, we have become very good at crisis. Our families give us sympathy. Our friends loan us money, help us move, call us up to see how we're doing, volunteer to buy us coffee. We feel safe, cared about, cared for. With this help and support, we feel competent and confident enough to start again.

Starting again, we set the sails, set our course, sail along smoothly until. . . .

Until we just have to capsize our lives.

Creating a crisis.

Many years ago, Julia, working as a free-lance writer, got an unexpected check for writing a low-budget movie. This was a big break for her: the movies. She'd always wanted to be a screenwriter. For starters, she got a whopping check for $8,000. She needed to live four months on it. It was just enough to get her through a first draft of the movie she'd taken on. She'd get another $8,000 on delivery, another for "polishes" later.

Coming, as it did, at a time when the free-lance income was low, the job seemed ideal, the money about right. She could rest easily, work calmly. All she needed was a few things for the house.

Three weeks later, Julia had Oriental rugs on the floor of every room, a Victorian sideboard, two oil paintings ("good florals"), and an entire movie left to write with no money to live on.

This wild, and uncharacteristic, over-spending on Julia's part is a perfect example of the cunning and slippery nature of the money disease. Here, her addiction was wearing the mask of the Compulsive Spender. While you might view this as a reaction to her recent deprivation, Julia insists it is far more likely that her real addiction was to adrenaline, worry, and discomfort. She simply had to be financially off-center one way or another. We have many times witnessed just such role reversals among the money drunk types.

"You had to do it," her brother teased her. "Solvency was about to rear its ugly head." In Julia's early years as an artist, her money mismanagement was the stuff of family legend. Either she was poor as a church mouse or living like a queen. The middle ground was terra incognita on her emotional map.

Julia recalls, "I got that job and I got that check and they *both* scared me. I told myself, if I got the house together a little I'd feel more secure, so I decided to buy a rug, sew some curtains."

Julia laughs now but writing that movie on pots of split pea soup and rice was no joke.

"They were going to turn off my electricity and my typewriter was electric!" she remembers. "I had a new tufted ottoman to rest my feet on, and had to use both sides of my typing paper . . ."

Everyone should know how to handle success, right? You just accept it. You just enjoy it. You just let it happen. It's no big deal, right?

Wrong.

On a stress scale, a promotion carries as much stress as getting fired. Yes. A promotion can be as stressful as getting fired. The psychological and physiological reactions are the same. Change for the better and change for the worse . . . both are still change. Both are still stress.

The success stress, the unseen enemy, can lead to illness, destructive behavior, and "acting out" in much the same way that the stress of failure can. Those of us money drunks who are also addicted in other ways may abruptly find ourselves battling the old urges to drink, to drug, to binge on food or sex or television.

Until we see our success as something to prepare for, we may trigger a celebration that could sabotage the rest of our work week or our recovery. Remember:

Progress, not perfection. It always takes a money drunk some time to sober up.

---

**ACTIVITIES**

1. List at least five "telltale signs" that might signal a relapse for you.

EXAMPLE: I don't open my mail.

EXAMPLE: I revert to "impulse buying" at the checkout.

**2.** List the times perfectionism has ambushed you into despair.

EXAMPLE: I lost my counting notebook and gave up for a week.

**3.** List the times when complacency ambushed you into backsliding.

EXAMPLE: I stopped writing my money down at the same time. I spent it and tried to "reconstruct" later.

**4.** List the stressors that trigger the itch to abuse your money.

EXAMPLE: Every time I fight with my spouse, I want a treat to cheer me up.

EXAMPLE: Every time I agree to go out with Jerry I believe I need a new dress to feel "passable."

EXAMPLE: Every time my family badmouths me I want to binge spend.

EXAMPLE: Whenever I am "waiting" for a deal, I want to buy an extravagant meal.

**5.** List five "upkeep" activities that signal you are in fact on the road to recovery.

EXAMPLE: I am doing my counting.

EXAMPLE: I open my mail promptly.

**6.** Make a gratitude list of everything you can think of.

**7.** Look up five words on the list of financial terms in this section. Helps get rid of inferiority.

**8.** Visit a financial institution (board of trade, brokerage office, bank, stock exchange, state building, or municipal city hall). Demystifies the place.

**9.** Practice your math skills with a calculator.

**10.** Watch a financial news network or CNN's "Moneyline" for a week. Helps us get more fluent with the big picture.

**11.** Read the *Wall Street Journal.* It's a good paper.

**12.** Play Monopoly. Recovery should be fun, remember?

**13.** Get a subscription to *Consumer Reports* or their annual buyers guide.

**14.** Buy a dictionary. Look up the words you don't know. Use it whenever you don't understand the meaning of a word or concept.

**15.** Compile your own shopper's safety list. (Example follows.) Keep adding to it.

**16.** Make the essentials list for your ideal home. Go shopping for it. Talk to the real estate agent about mortgages and what is possible for you in your income range.

**17.** Make the essentials list for your next car. Go shopping.

**18.** Make the essentials list for whatever else you are thinking you might buy soon, such as computer, stereo, television, couch. Use your prosperity plan to figure how long it will take to have it. Think of ways you could get it cheaper. (For example, we bought a 286 computer because it fulfills our essentials list but is not as expensive as a 386 or 486.)

## A Shopper's Safety List

1. Always get at least two prices on everything.

2. Wait 24 hours before buying anything major. *Never* buy anything on impulse.

3. On large items, analyze your expected return on investment.

4. Discover the "essentials" of what you want. For instance, if you are buying a car, what kind do you want? What

should it do for you? Many of our students have found older cars that are top of the line but have a few miles on them to be great buys. Of course, take it to two mechanics to get it checked out before buying.

5. Always shop for prices *and* quality. Try to compare apples to apples. In other words, when clothes shopping for instance, you might like a shirt that costs $50 and decide to get one that costs $40, only to find out that the $40 is not of pure cotton but a blend.

# SPIRITUALITY: THE RECOVERY OF PEACE

For many recovering money drunks, it is very difficult to link money and spirituality. Like most Westerners, we tend to unconsciously believe in a dualistic world: spirit *versus* matter.

As we see it, there are two different realms, one Godly and one apart from God. Believing this way, in the spiritual versus the material, we are understandably reluctant to seek spiritual guidance in our financial affairs. God just might advise us to give all our worldly goods to the poor and take a vow of poverty.

In working with the idea of a spiritual recovery from a financial illness, we often find our "God concept" must come in for a major overhaul. Exactly what kind of God do we believe in? For most of us, it is the God we were taught to believe in when we were young. Inherited from *our* parents, perhaps inherited from *their* parents, such a God is often a grim taskmaster, officially "kind" but actually rather stern and conservative where money is concerned.

It's little wonder that with a God like that most money drunks keep their financial dealings to themselves.

"First I had to admit I'd been blaming God for my being broke all those years," says Sean, a recovering money drunk. "Then I had to admit that even with blaming God, I had never once asked God for any help or guidance. 'I can do it myself' was my credo. Kind of 'God helps those that help themselves' but without the God part."

"God doesn't do business," Natasha, a recovering money drunk states, pinpointing the sticking point in her recovery. No longer debting, even whittling away at her debts one day at a time, Natasha still has a hard time trusting her future well-being to a loving God.

Raised in a conventional Protestant home, she was taught that God was "otherworldly," disinterested in and a little disapproving of our human affairs. While acknowledging her finances to be unmanageable ("scary" is the word Natasha uses), she doesn't really accept or invite spiritual help in sorting them out.

What kind of God would "do" money? Is it possible for us to trust in, or at least explore, the possibility of a God concept differing from our parents'?

Why not focus on the God who says, "All Good shall come to him whose mind is stayed on me." We money drunks need to ask these questions. Could we believe in a God (or a God Force) that took a benevolent interest in the unfolding of our financial schemes?

"As within, so without," the spiritual adage goes, and many recovering money drunks have discovered that by doing the inner work of altering their God concept with prayer and meditation into a benevolent one, they have experienced a softening and quickening in their outer affairs as well.

For the rationalists among us, the idea of a benevolent force active in human affairs meets with immediate resistance. "Prove it," we want to say. We would urge such rationalists to try proving it themselves. Many of us have entered into a spiritual collaboration in the spirit of scientific inquiry. Imagine our startled skepticism when such spiritual forays bore financial and emotional fruit!

Before we go any further, we would like to take a look at what it is that causes so many of us such great resistance when we think about inviting spiritual guidance into our fiscal concerns. Make no mistake, this is an idea that makes very many of us *very* nervous; even those of us who have tried relying on God as a partner and guide often find we would still rather "go it alone" where our money is concerned. Like Natasha, we may believe God doesn't "do" money. And if our God *is* money, there is never enough.

For a money drunk, God is unnecessary. Only cash fixes anything. To a money drunk, money doesn't talk, it shouts, in the universal language of greed. From Beijing to Boston, cash is king.

Even God, it seems, requires a dollar in the basket every Sunday. "It's a good deal, absolution for a buck, and God must be pretty dumb to make such easy terms. And besides, if the world he made has gone so bankrupt, what does that say about God?" runs our diatribe.

Closeminded on spiritual matters, we money drunks point defensively to the shortcomings of "spiritual" people and institutions. Deriding television evangelists with million-dollar lifestyles is one of our specialties. Wanting more of the "good life" ourselves, it galls us to see glitz and excess that is not our own.

With cash in hand, who needs a God?

As practicing money drunks, we don't need God—we are God. We've got the power, buying power. When we buy a round at the bar after work, we're not just a big spender, we're a big shot, more potent than the booze in our beer and chaser. It's a matter of perspective; with a little cash to throw around, our problems become smaller and we become big enough to handle them. We become big enough to deserve respect.

To a money drunk, respect is something we have to earn from others, and like money, there is never enough. We are greedy. There is that God-shaped hole in our heart. No matter how much money we pour into it, the center will not hold.

Barry remembers a time before he sought help for his insolvency: "I got my first monogrammed shirts. They reminded me of when I was in high school and it was very important to wear a Gant or an Eagle shirt. Kids in my class would look at each other's shirt labels. I worked overtime bagging groceries to pay for my Gants. Then, ten years later, I found myself pulling my shirt cuffs down below my jacket sleeve so that the monogram showed. I would ride the bus or train downtown and hold the strap with the monogram showing. Now, years into recovery, I laugh at the thought of trying to impress anyone with the labels on my clothes."

As Barry knows, the "God-shaped" hole inside must be filled from within. We must learn to love, nurture, and value ourselves. Then the phrase "dig deep" won't make us think of our pockets.

Most of us need help to do this. We may need fellowship, prayer, reparenting, professional counseling—often a combination of all four. Now we are building a foundation of inner strength, a reserve of self-respect. As we learn to reach "within" more and more frequently, we sense a transcendent power. We get a glimpse of Grace.

Grace: "The unmerited divine assistance for humankind's sanctification."

Sanctification: "To be set aside for a special purpose."

These are old-fashioned words for what may be a brand-new experience. It is easy to say there is no God until you experiment and find one.

Gloria laughs remembering her first encounter with the power within. "I had gone to my favorite bookstore, checkbook in hand. I'd just had a fight with my boyfriend and I was going to get a book to fix us and to fix how rotten I was feeling."

"I had six dollars cash and my checkbook in my purse. If I wrote a check, it would bounce, but that never stopped me before. My banker was understanding. I began stacking up books, lots of books, not just the one I had come for. They were all good books, but I was buying them because I felt bad. Suddenly, I remembered to pray. I asked for help quietly under my breath."

"By now, I was writing the check. The salesman had rung the sale. 'Stop,' I said. 'I only really need the first book.' I thought the salesman would be angry. He was more amused. I paid cash for the book and went home lighthearted. I couldn't believe it. Prayer had worked."

You may not call it God. Gloria didn't, and you don't have to. What you call it doesn't matter. *That* you call on it, does. As we let go of the hunger for external acquisitions, we begin to acquire inner wealth. This is not often easy when we grew up in money-drunk homes.

"God is not going to come down and put food on your table," Mac's father used to scream at the family. "When is the last time you saw God pay the rent?" was another often-heard refrain.

Mac is a recovering money drunk. He knows that self-reliance failed him in his financial dealings but he still has a very hard time with the "God idea." He traces this difficulty back to his father's attitude.

"I guess he meant God really isn't much use for anything practical," Mac says. "Our mother tried to keep us in Sunday school and church and she made sure each of us was baptized, but Dad made sure we wouldn't rely on God for anything, daily bread or otherwise."

Mac continues, "Even now it is hard for me to get the idea that 'God will provide.' I can always hear my father telling me he won't."

One day just after he "bottomed out" about his finances and became willing to "go to any lengths" to get financially sober, Mac asked God for help to humbly share his *real* financial situation with others. This humility landed him in a discussion with his sponsor.

Mac's sponsor asked him: "How many days have you been alive?

Mac thought over his 35 years at 365 days a year and answered, "Somewhere over ten thousand I guess."

And Mac's sponsor said, "Mac, if you had a business supplier who had delivered to you everything you needed for over ten thousand days in a row, wouldn't you feel pretty sure that he would deliver what you need for today?"

Mac's eyes filled with tears as he suddenly understood a phrase he had heard at AA meetings for many years:

"We will suddenly realize that God is doing for us what we could not do for ourselves."

And looking back over his life, and his years in recovery, he suddenly knew in his heart that it was true. This realization is often at the core of a spiritual awakening. It is that feeling when we suddenly know we are all right and at peace. Since many of us have made money our God, this inner, numinous experience is one we deny ourselves. Focused on the future, we are unable to experience what is called the eternal now with its sense of safety and of wonder. In the *now* we are always enough. This was the beginnings of faith for Mac and the start of a renewed commitment to himself to keep working for solvency.

With a seed of faith, self-worth becomes internal, something solid we can bank on. Instead of needing "labels" to demonstrate our worth, we learn to love ourselves without them. Within the borders of our hearts, our credit's good again. We don't sell ourselves short. We don't cheat ourselves or fudge our accounts. Back from the abyss of spiritual bankruptcy, we count our blessings and our change.

## AFFIRMATIONS

As recovering money drunks, we need to learn to think and feel differently. For many of us, affirmations have proven to be a valuable tool. We write them out when we are nervous. We say them daily during our "quiet time."

At first, many of us found them silly or even repellent in their optimism. "This is brainwashing." "This is bull . . .," we protested. Later, we learned to admit, "Maybe my brain *needed* some washing." It is not necessary to have the word *God* in an affirmation; just write one of your own that states what you want in positive terms. (For example, "I am prosperous and wise in many matters.")

We suggest you write the affirmation several times each morning and say it out loud while writing it. Many of our students like to carry a copy of the affirmation in their pocket and say it over and over again during the day. The point is to make it a habit of daily practice and also to use them when things are rough.

Practice using the affirmations below.

---

### AFFIRMATIONS FOR THE COMPULSIVE SPENDER

1. I allow God to guide my spending.

2. I spend in appropriate ways.

3. I spend only as I need.

4. I allow myself to shop moderately.

5. I buy wisely.

## Affirmations for the Big Deal Chaser

1. I see money as a means to an end.
2. I have worth in and of myself.
3. I see the worth in all others.
4. I live fruitfully in the present.
5. I bloom where I am planted.

## Affirmations for the Maintenance Money Drunk

1. Money is energy and I allow it to flow.
2. Money serves me and I use it wisely.
3. Money circulates freely through my life and my affairs.
4. I accept financial good and let go my fears of abundance.
5. Money comes to me from many channels and I accept them all.
6. God is the source of my good.
7. Money is solid energy and nothing more.

## Affirmations for the Poverty Addict

1. I allow abundance into my life.
2. I accept comfort in my life.
3. My abundance allows others to prosper.
4. Comfort allows me to prosper spiritually.
5. I accept more ease in my life.
6. I allow financial abundance.

## AFFIRMATIONS FOR THE CASH CO-DEPENDENT

1. My finances are my own.

2. I am only responsible for my income.

3. My own dreams deserve my financial backing.

4. My finances are mine to control.

5. My money is mine to use for me.

6. I am allowed to say yes to me and no to others.

## AFFIRMATIONS FOR MANAGEABILITY

1. I use money wisely.

2. I think clearly in financial dealings.

3. I spend money usefully.

4. I allow myself financial clarity.

5. I choose wisely in financial matters.

## AFFIRMATIONS FOR PROSPERITY PLANNING

1. My good comes from many sources.

2. My finances prosper under God's care.

3. My abundance reflects my openness to God's abundance.

4. I open my life and invite abundance.

5. I receive good gratefully.

## AFFIRMATIONS TO AVOID RELAPSE

1. I remember to be guided in financial matters.

2. I trust my inner voice to guide me.

3. I accept God's help from many human sources.

4. God can restore me to financial sanity.

5. God's power and wisdom overmatches any calamity.

### AFFIRMATIONS FOR ESTABLISHING SPIRITUAL CONTACT

1. I allow God to establish my well-being.

2. I accept divine guidance in my worldly affairs.

3. I draw on divine goodness to fulfill my earthly plans.

4. My dreams come from God, who unfolds them through me.

5. I accept God's help in all money matters.

---

**ACTIVITIES**

1. Read this Morning Prayer every day for a week:
   My creator, you are the source of my supply. I entrust to you my financial well-being. Please guide me today to take appropriate actions. Please plan for me—and with me—a prosperous day. Help me to remember I am a channel for your good. Show me ways to be useful, fruitful, thoughtful of others. Guide me, please, to a balance between work and play, work and pay, love for myself and others, and this day you have given me. Amen.

2. Write your own prayer.

3. Create an image file for yourself. Choose images that remind you instantly of the abundant powers of God. Waterfalls, the ocean, a field of flowers, a starry night, the Grand Canyon. You have asked this power to help you.

**4.** Create a "sacred space" in your environment. This needn't be a whole room or even a whole part of one. A shelf will do, a little table, even a corner. What matters is that you dedicate this space to enriching your spiritual connection. Many of us use a candle, incense, fresh flowers, or rocks—things of beauty that awaken our sense of wonder.

**5.** Spend 10 minutes daily at your sacred space. You may wish to use your affirmations there.

**6.** What is your "God concept?" Does your God "do" money? Write in your journal on this and questions 7–10; it will aid in clarifying your thinking.

**7.** What did your family religion teach you about God and money?

**8.** What does your God believe about money?

**9.** Does any alternative God concept appeal to you?

**10.** Are you willing to pray for monetary guidance? (If not, then don't, use secular affirmations and the other tools.)

**11.** Take a walk around your neighborhood. Walking is a great way to get in touch with how we feel.

## Vision:
## THE
## RECOVERY
## OF HOPE

These are the last few days of the 90-day program. By now you have probably made considerable progress and are beginning to feel excited about your future. With your money addiction safely in check, many things begin to seem possible: returning to school, owning a home, traveling around the world. We urge you to congratulate yourself on your progress to date and to remember that prosperity is a process, an ever-unfolding process.

At the end of this chapter you will inventory and consolidate the gains you have made so far and recommit to using the tools for further progress. Within the safety of a firm commitment to continued solvency, your vision for a prosperous future will take even deeper hold. It is our belief that these hopes for the future mature as we do.

When we are children we have so many dreams. We want to be so many things when we grow up—a pilot, a doctor, a nurse, a fireman, an astronaut. Maybe even president. Mark had a friend, Eddie, who wanted to be king, and he used to joke "at least czar of the southeast sector." An interesting political joke from a 12-year-old.

Our hopes are sky high at that age; as children we want so much for ourselves, for our families. Many of us actually think we could be president, or something better. We envision ourselves doing wonderful things, curing cancer, ending war, helping the sick, taking care of animals, feeding the hungry, learning our father's trade, being a good mother. In working with adolescents, we find many that want to take care of Grandma, make their parents proud of them, stop the fighting in their house, make their parents love each other. So many noble goals and high aspirations.

Then life moves along.

An old Chinese proverb says that life is like a ball of twine unraveling. You can throw the twine in a general direction but no one can predict how it will unwind. No doubt such is the same for most of us. Childhood visions of who we will be when we grow up come head to head with our limitations, personal, familial, even political.

Our grades in school may not be as high as we would hope. Our family might not have the money to send us to college—we have to work our way through, or not go at all. Maybe our family loves us but doesn't know how to teach us what we need to know. Maybe early childhood trauma catches up with us and by 16 we are acting out and getting in trouble in ways that we later regret. Or, like Mark's friend Eddie, we get sabotaged by drug addiction that takes our life before we are 30, all of our dreams dead.

For many of us, facing the loss of our dreams has led us to coping mechanisms that have been as difficult to control as that ball of twine—addictions to alcohol, to other drugs, to food or other physical self-abuse, to financial mismanagement and the money addiction. All of them damaging and all of them attempts at maintaining a sense of possibility in our lives.

The drinker shoots back a shot of whiskey and for a time just might be able to be president again. The sex addict becomes king and, like Eddie's dream, is adored by loyal subjects, if only for a few minutes. The food addict sneaks a few Twinkies and in the lull of the sugar high is suddenly safe and living with a family that loves one another and loves him too. And the money drunk can get lost in overtime or spending or the big deal so that she doesn't have to face the scary proposition of intimacy, of talking to a husband who may not love her, of trying to feel smart enough or kind enough or loving enough to say the perfect thing to her children so that they will grow up to be good. Maybe the Poverty Addict lives so dutifully in austere sainthood that her dead mother will notice that she really is a good little girl who wants to make her mommy proud.

As practicing money drunks, we are tangled in our ball of twine, unable to extricate ourselves from our tangled, mangled dreams. In solvency, our vision clears. We begin to untangle our knotted affairs. We see ourselves and our lives more clearly. We focus first on clearing the wreckage and then, as solvency grows, we often find ourselves facing an open horizon for the first time in years. On that horizon of hope, we envision a future.

Initially, this vision is usually modest: we want to be able to pay our rent on time, repair our car, keep a steady flow of groceries, and buy a few new clothes. As solvency progresses, so does our vision. Many of us feel we are coming out of the fog in an ever-progressive way. We stop focusing on our near future and lift our heads to a more distant horizon, to where our dreams once shimmered.

For many of us, the thought of dreaming again is frightening. We want to be safe and secure. We are glad the storm is over but we feel safer lurking below ground in our fallout shelter rather than venturing above ground to build a new and sturdier home.

It is our experience that in solvency we stop hiding—and hiding from—our dreams and our talents. We have found that in recovery it is possible to dream safely and on an ever-broader scale.

We are not suggesting that all of us should dream in capital letters, fantasizing feudal kingdoms to run. What we are saying is that our vision gradually expands to include not only safety and security but also aspirations, hopes, and dreams. Christ said, unless you become like little children, you will not enter the kingdom of heaven. Perhaps our visions are an attempt to do exactly that, to enter the kingdom. "With God and solvency, all things are possible," we have come to feel.

Many of us did not want to end up as we did at our bottom from some addiction. Trapped by old unworkable notions of who we were, we didn't plan to end up year after year owing more and owning less; working harder and hating ourselves more. Becoming, over time, cynical, bitter, and resentful instead of happy, loving, and free.

Maybe the financial and moral bankruptcy of our addiction is the disguised opportunity to send us back to be like children, with dreams as big as our imaginations can invent. Whether you picture it as a tangled ball of yarn or a mountain of financial wreckage, we assure you: You are larger than your money problems; you can grow bigger than they are.

Allow yourself to dream: Maybe there really is a way out of darkness and back into the truth and the light. Part of what becomes possible is envisioning not only a fiscal ideal but also a spiritual ideal. As we settle our debts and stabilize our finances, many of us find an inner hunger to invest not only in financial betterment but also personal growth. We go back to school, undertake career shifts, apply for grants.

As our cynicism wears thin, many of us find an attraction to service, to dreams that look suspiciously close to those we had as kids. Humbled by our addiction, we find glory in our childhood dreams of helping—like the child wearing the nurse's hat or playing teacher to her younger siblings.

Now we can dream our dreams of childhood again and couple them with the knowledge and tools of the wise. We may not be an astronaut but we could learn to fly. Maybe not a doctor, but we can volunteer at a local hospital. Maybe not president, but we can know right from wrong and practice it ourselves. Maybe not make our families love one another but we can learn to love them and ourselves.

Your vision can be anything: a college degree, your own home, a car, clothes that fit, world peace. Many of us started with a simple vision of our rent paid and food on the table. The vision changed. It grew.

Visions are as powerful and as progressive as the addiction. That is the one great gift God gave us. We can be much, we can have much, one step at a time, one day at a time, starting right now.

If your vision of your future is fear, you will let go of it. If it is so confused that you cannot even see what you want, don't worry, the path becomes clearer. Starting with your vision can be as simple as listing 10 things you would like to have/do/be. Revise this list in a month's time, or six months' time, crossing off the items fulfilled. We call this a Wish List. As ephemeral as it sounds, many of us have experienced our wishes as accomplished facts.

Matthew has gone back to college and graduates in June. Gary has paid his taxes and even managed to buy a hang glider. Charley has written his first novel and started a second. Michelle has lightened her caseload as an attorney and begun her own radio show. Kathy has raised her fees and starts graduate school soon. We ourselves have moved from the city to the country and are finishing this work in a home that was a wish only a year ago.

It was part of our vision, as we became money sober, to share our tools with others through a book. It is our hope that it will become part of your vision to share the tools with still others because of their success for you.

To some of you, this may not sound possible. We assure you that it is. Mark insists we end this book as we always end our classes, with the legend of Edmund Hillary, a visionary extraordinaire. As a boy he was a beekeeper in New Zealand who dreamed of climbing Mount Everest. Years later, as a man, he tried Everest and failed. Many men before him had died trying. Defeated, Hillary faced his backers, the London Explorers' Club, who in a sense had lost everything.

As Hillary stood at the podium in front of a projected picture of Everest, he suddenly turned and said: "I will defeat you Everest, because you cannot get any bigger—and I can."

Hillary defeated Everest in May 1953 and was knighted in July, that same year.

---

### ACTIVITIES

**1.** Make a wish list of all the things you would like to HAVE. (New car, home, savings account, new suit.) Shop for one without buying.

**2.** Make a wish list of all the things you would like to DO. (Travel, ski, horseback ride, spend a weekend in the country.) Do one as a present to yourself. Make sure it fits your Prosperity Plan.

**3.** Make a wish list of all the things you would like to BE. (College graduate, pilot, dancer, musician.) Take an action on your behalf.

**4.** Have BEING and DOING become more important than HAVING? This is a shift that happens to many of us as materialism loses its hold.

**5.** Make a positive inventory of the areas in which you have stabilized and improved over the last 3 months.

**6.** Start another 90 days. See if it is any easier. It will be.

---

## GOOD LUCK AND GOD BLESS

# BIBLIOGRAPHY

The following bibliography includes some of our personal favorites. These books represent some of the very best in their field.

*Al-Anon's Twelve Steps and Twelve Traditions.* New York: Al-Anon Family Group Headquarters, Inc., 1981. (Excellent for the Cash Co-Dependent).

*Alcoholics Anonymous.* 3rd ed. New York: Alcoholics Anonymous World Services, Inc., 1976. (The cornerstone of the recovery movement, this book brought hope and a language of spiritual healing to millions.)

BEATTIE, MELODY. *Beyond Codependency.* San Francisco: Harper and Row, 1989. (Excellent for understanding relapse behaviors).

BECKER, ERNEST. *The Denial of Death.* New York: The Free Press, 1973. (Great book about the roots of fear).

BERRY, CARMEN RENEE. *When Helping You Is Hurting Me.* San Francisco: Harper and Row, 1988. (Must reading for the Cash Co-Dependent).

BLACK, CLAUDIA. *It Will Never Happen To Me!* Denver: M.A.C., 1985. (Explains multigenerational alcoholic family dynamics).

BOLEN, JEAN SHINODA. *The Tao of Psychology.* San Francisco: Harper and Row, 1979. (An excellent jumping-off point for spiritual seekers).

BRADSHAW, JOHN. *Healing the Shame That Binds You.* Pompano Beach, Fla.: Health Communications, 1987. (Superb book for explaining the role of shame in the addiction process).

BUTTERWORTH, ERIC. *Spiritual Economics: The Prosperity Process.* Unity Village, Mo.: Unity School Of Christianity, 1983. (Interesting explanation of prosperity as a spiritual issue).

*Came to Believe.* New York: Alcoholics Anonymous World Services, Inc., 1973. (Useful and touching book about embryonic faith).

CAMERON, JULIA. *The Artist's Way.* Los Angeles: Jeremy P. Tarcher, Inc., 1992. (A spiritual guide to recovering/discovering creativity.)

COLGROVE, MELBA; BLOOMFIELD, HAROLD; MCWILLIAM, PETER. *How To Survive the Loss of a Love.* New York: Leo Press/Simon and Schuster, 1976. (Helpful pointers for self-nurturing during withdrawal phase).

FIELDS, RICK; TAYLOR, PEGGY; WEYLER, REX; AND INGRASCI, RICK. *Chop Wood Carry Water.* Los Angeles: Jeremy P. Tarcher, Inc., 1984. (Excellent for finding dignity in our daily work. It is an inviting overview of synthesis of East/West spirituality.)

*Living Sober.* New York: Alcoholics Anonymous World Services, Inc., 1975. (Invaluable in the early withdrawal phases of recovery.)

MUNDIS, JERROLD. *How to Get Out of Debt, Stay Out of Debt, and Live Prosperously.* New York: Bantam Books, 1988. (The first and best "tool" guide for Debtors Anonymous recovery. Highly recommended).

NORWOOD, ROBIN. *Women Who Love Too Much.* Los Angeles: Jeremy P. Tarcher, Inc., 1985. (Seminal work on co-dependency. Excellent for Cash Co-Dependents.)

ORSBORN, CAROL. *Enough is Enough: Exploding the Myth of Having It All.* New York: G. P. Putnam's Sons, 1986. (Excellent for helping dismantle the "heroic" addictive personality).

PECK, M. SCOTT. *The Road Less Traveled.* New York: Simon and Schuster, 1978. (A book for early spiritual skeptics.)

*Sex and Love Addicts Anonymous.* Boston: The Augustine Fellowship, Sex and Love Addicts Anonymous Fellowship-Wide Services, Inc., 1986. (One of the best books on addiction. The withdrawal and building partnerships chapters should be required reading.)

*The Little Red Book.* Center City, Minn.: Hazelden, 1970. (The pocket driver's manual for recovery.)

*Twelve Steps and Twelve Traditions.* New York: Alcoholics Anonymous World Services, Inc., 1952. (This book is a spiritual toolkit. Another must read.)

WINN, MARIE. *The Plug in Drug: Television, Children, and the Family.* New York: Viking-Penguin Books, 1977. (Necessary reading for all suspected TV addicts and parents.)

# INDEX

Abstinence, from incurring debts,
56, 57, 123–131
Accuracy, recovery of, 143–147
Addiction to money. *See* Money
addiction; Money drunks
Addictive patterns
intertwined, 22, 68–69
recognition of, 7–8
Affirmations, 205–208
to avoid relapse, 107–108
for Big Deal Chasers, 206
for Cash Co-Dependents, 207
for Compulsive Spenders, 205
for establishing spiritual
contact, 208
for Maintenance Money
Drunks, 206
for manageability, 207
for Poverty Addicts, 206
for prosperity planning, 207
Alcoholics Anonymous, 111, 152
American Dream, 82
Anger, 29–30, 125–130
constructive use of, 127, 130
in recovery, 125–130
right to feel, 86
Anorexia, 25
financial, 25 (*see also* Poverty
Addicts; Self-denial)

Balance, recovery of, 139–142
Big Deal Chasers, 9, 26, 32, 61–79
affirmations for, 206
belief system of, 62–63, 83
bottoming out for, 70–71
Cash Co-Dependents and, 99–100
limit-setting in recovery, 141
and magic numbers, 64–65, 71

questions for self-diagnosis,
78–79
recovery for, 71–78
self-esteem of, 64–69, 71
self-image of, 73
workaholics as, 65–67
Big Payoff, 26
Binge spending, 8, 15, 186
Borrowing, 140
by Big Deal Chasers, 74–75
Bottom, hitting, 27–28, 29–30
for Big Deal Chaser, 70–71
Bottom line. *See* Limit-setting
Boundaries, difficulty in establishing,
46–47
Buddies. *See* Money buddies
Burnout, avoiding, 179

Caretaking, financial, of parents,
46–47
Cash Co-Dependents, 9, 32, 99–107
accepting role in money addiction
cycle, 102–104
affirmations for, 207
limit-setting in recovery, 141
questions for self-diagnosis,
106–107
recovery of, 104–106, 127–129
self-esteem of, 103
support groups for, 105
Change, stress of, 192, 195
Childhood experiences, 35–48. *See
also* Family patterns; Parents
questions regarding, 47–48
Childhood visions, 214
Clarity, recovery of, 117–121
Co-Dependents. *See* Cash
Co-Dependents

221

# ABOUT THE
# AUTHORS

Mark Bryan is a seasoned teacher, writer, and business consultant. He has taught free enterprise in Russia as a guest of the Russian Government and is the creator of "Business Creativity," a seminar on creativity in the world of business. Currently Bryan is Senior Counselor at Aspen Meadows Psychiatric Hospital, Velarde, New Mexico, and is at work on a new book about family reunification for fathers who have left children and the children they have left behind.

Julia Cameron is an award-winning writer and filmmaker with extensive credits in journalism, film and television. She has written for the *New York Times*, *Washington Post*, *Chicago Tribune*, and *Los Angeles Times* as well as many national magazines. She has taught writing and creativity for many years, most recently serving as Writer-in-Residence, Northwestern University. Privately, Cameron teaches the autobiographical seminar, "The Vein of Gold." She is also the author of *The Artist's Way*, a book on discovering and recovering the creative self.

Together, the authors form the creative partnership, Power and Light, Inc. and are currently serving on the faculty of the

College of Santa Fe, Santa Fe, New Mexico. Bryan and Cameron teach seminars and workshops on their 90-day program for money drunks and on creativity based on *The Artist's Way*.

For information regarding seminars, workshops and other books by the authors, write to:

Power and Light
P.O. Box 1423
Ranchos de Taos,
NM 87557.